A Concise Guide to SSL/TLS for DevOps

2nd Edition 2017

A Concise Guide to SSL/TLS for DevOps

Introduction to this book

This book, the 2nd edition of 'A Concise Guide to SSL/TLS for DevOps' is like the original an introduction to SSL & TLS in application and operational environments and as such is a more technical in depth study than is typically the case in the Executive and Management series. However this edition has undergone extensive rewriting and additional material has been added to cover cryptography, troubleshooting and to generally update the book for 2017. This book still aims to cover the theory and practice of SSL in working operational situations. Consequently, although no prior knowledge of authentication and encryption methods is required, a good deal of this text will involve encryption theory and certificate management.

What is DevOps?

The practice of DevOps is a new term in IT and Operations that has emerging from the amalgamation of two major related practices. Indeed, the first tentative steps to consolidate IT, development and systems operations, was called, "agile system administration" or "agile operations". This term springs from application and software development life cycle and is the flexible, agile way of developing application software. The idea being that IT could develop by applying newer Agile and Lean approaches to not just development but to operation's work procedures. Consequently, efforts in development became more focused on collaboration between planning, implementation and operations whereas before there had been conflict. Furthermore, IT staff, throughout all stages of the development lifecycle, when creating, deploying and operating a service, now understands the importance of cross-function collaboration.

A good definition of DevOps:

DevOps is the practice where operations and development engineers are participating together in the entire service lifecycle, from design through the development process to production support.

What is SSL/TLS?

SSL is the secure communications protocol of choice for secure internet transactions. There are many applications of SSL, since it provides both web server authentication and a method of securing any transmission over TCP. Secure HTTP, or HTTPS, that little padlock in the address bar is a familiar application of SSL in e-commerce or internet banking applications.

According to the Internet Draft of the SSL Protocol, the purpose of SSL "is to provide privacy and reliability between two communicating applications." The protocol release further explains that three points combine to provide connection security:

- Privacy – SSL provides a secure connection through encryption
- Identity authentication – SSL provides server side identification through certificates
- Reliability – SSL provides dependable maintenance of a secure connection through message integrity checking.

The current version of SSL is version 3.0, and Netscape released this way back in 1999. However, today we do not use SSL, even though the name has stuck, we actually now use TLS. Furthermore although SSLv3.0 and all of its siblings are still found in the wild all of them have been deprecated and banned from use in today's TLS secure world. This is because the Internet Engineering Task Force (IETF) created a similar protocol in an attempt to standardize SSL within the Internet community. This protocol became the Transport Layer Security (TLS) protocol version 1.0 and today we are now on the latest version of TLS v1.2.

Both TLS and its predecessor SSL provide the security principles of secure key exchange, authentication, encryption and integrity hence their utility in securing sensitive web-based transactions. For example in ecommerce SSL has been providing authenticate of web servers for twenty years now. Where once there was considerable doubt over the identity of a web server, as spoofing server names and URL identities was and still is a common practice. However with the advent of SSL a client was able to connect and communicating with confidence with any SSL enabled web server across the Web.

An SSL/TLS server authenticates itself to a client that is wishing to establish a session by the use of an SSL certificate. If you consider the following scenario, it shows a common application of SSL:

A user wishes to connect from their mobile phone's browser to an email server, so that they can check their mail. Now, it is important to the user that the email server's identity is authenticated before they pass over their user name and password credentials. However, to the server it doesn't matter what the connecting client device is as the user can login from any device. Therefore from the email application's and web server's perspective they only require the user's login credentials. On the other hand, the server does need to authenticate to the client device during the SSL session initiation. Hence, the server uses an SSL certificate that has been issued by a trusted authority, which as it is trusted by both parties serves to authenticates the server as being genuine.

Overview of SSL

To understand how SSL/TLS works we need to first take a look as to where it is situated in the TCP protocol stack. The name TLS or Transport Layer Service provides a large clue to the fact that SSL/TLS acts as a transport protocol for the higher level application protocols.

TCP/IP governs the transport and routing of data over the Internet. Other protocols, such as the HTTP, LDAP, or SMTP use TCP/IP to support typical application tasks such as displaying web pages or running mail servers.

Figure 1–1 Where SSL Runs

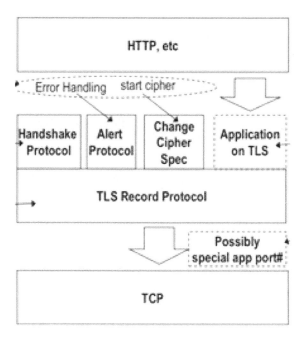

The SSL protocol runs above TCP/IP and below higher-level protocols such as HTTP or IMAP. This is in network terms is called the transport layer and this layer interacts with TCP/IP on behalf of the higher-level protocols. By operating as an intermediate between the applications and the network TCP/IP protocols SSL/TLS allows an SSL-enabled server to authenticate itself to an SSL-enabled client, and simultaneously allows the client – if required - to authenticate itself to the server, so that both machines can establish an encrypted connection.

SSL addresses the following concerns about communication over the Internet and other TCP/IP networks:

- SSL server authentication allows a user to confirm a server's identity.

- SSL-enabled client software can use standard techniques of public-key cryptography to check that a server's certificate and public ID are valid and have been issued by a certificate authority (CA) listed in the client's list of trusted CAs. This confirmation might be important if the user, for example, is sending a credit card number over the network and wants to check the receiving server's identity.

- SSL client authentication allows a server to confirm a client's identity, though this is seldom used in today's highly mobile world where user's work from several client devices and supporting an SSL/TLS certificate on each would be neither desirable nor secure.

However, although not commonly implemented we should still be aware that in highly secure environments client side authentication is a possibility. By using the same techniques as those used for server authentication, SSL-enabled server software can check that a client's certificate and public ID are valid and have been issued by a certificate authority (CA) listed in the server's list of trusted CAs. This confirmation might be important if the server, for example, is a Bank, which is receiving confidential financial information or funds from a customer and wants reassurance of the sender's identity.

An encrypted SSL connection requires all information sent between a client and a server to be encrypted by the sending software and decrypted by the receiving software, thus providing a high degree of confidentiality.

Confidentiality is important for both parties to any private transaction. In addition, all data sent over an encrypted SSL connection is protected with a mechanism for detecting tampering—that is, for automatically determining whether the data has been altered in transit.

The SSL protocol includes two sub-protocols: the SSL record protocol and the SSL handshake protocol.

The SSL record protocol defines the format used to transmit data. The SSL handshake protocol involves using the SSL record protocol to exchange a series of messages between an SSL-enabled server and an SSL-enabled client when they first establish an SSL connection. This exchange of messages is designed to facilitate the following actions:

- Authenticate the server to the client.

- Allow the client and server to select the cryptographic algorithms, or ciphers, that they both support.

- Optionally authenticate the client to the server.

- Use public-key encryption techniques to generate shared secrets.

- Establish an encrypted SSL connection.

What is an SSL Certificate?

An SSL certificate is an X.509 digital certificate, which is actually a small piece of code that has been issued by a trusted authority that has two specific functions:

1. Authentication and Verification: The SSL certificate is a digital signature, which has specific information about the authenticity of certain details regarding the identity of the website. The client can visibly check this when they click on the browser's padlock symbol or trust mark.

2. Data Encryption: The SSL certificate also enables encryption, which means that the sensitive information exchanged between the client and the website cannot be read by anyone trying to intercept the traffic over the internet.

Of course, for this procedure to work then the SSL certificate must be issued by an authority of trust in the same way that a passport may only be issued by a country's government officials. Therefore only a trusted

Certificate Authority (CA) should issue an SSL certificate. The CA has to follow very strict rules and procedures in order to verify the identity of those wishing to obtain an SSL certificate. Therefore, it is not a trivial task to obtain an SSL certificate from a reputable trusted authority and will require proof of domain ownership, company registration, and even notarized company documentation for high trust certificates.

Every SSL certificate that a CA-verified entity issues, relates to a website domain (*a registered website address*). When a client uses their browser to navigate to the address of a website with an SSL certificate, an SSL handshake (*greeting*) occurs between the browser and server.
The client browser requests information regarding identity from the server in order to authenticate the websites authenticity. If there is a genuine SSL certificate installed on the server from a trusted third party CA, and that certificate has not expired then the website will be authenticated and the user will see this happening in their browser window – typically with a green lock or key in the URL bar. Should the browser detect a problem with the certificate or not recognize the trusted CA the browser will warn the user that it is unsafe to proceed.

However, in order to apply for an SSL certificate you must raise the required SSL CSR (certificate signing request) on the actual server where the certificate will be deployed. This used to be a requirement but is no longer the case. Despite this it is still a good idea to create the CSR on the server that the certificate will be deployed on as the process creates the private key – which we will see, is of vital importance and if it should be displaced or lost then the SSL certificate when it arrives will be useless.

Public Keys/Private Key

SSL uses a public key (Certificate) and a private key to encrypt information being transmitted, and this provides for confidentiality. Encryption using a private key/public key pair ensures that the data can be encrypted by one key, the public key but can only be decrypted by the private key pair. The keys are similar in nature and can be used alternatively: what one key encrypts, the other key pair can decrypt. The key pair is based on prime numbers and their length in terms of bits ensures the difficulty of being able to decrypt the message without the key pairs. The trick in a key pair is to keep one key secret (the private key) and to distribute the other key (the public key) to everybody. Anybody can send you an encrypted message using your public key that only you will be able to decrypt using your private key. In the opposite direction, you can certify that a message is only coming from you, because you have encrypted it with you private key, and only the associated public key will decrypt it correctly. Beware; however as in this case the message is not secured you have only signed it. This provides for non-repudiation but not confidentiality as everybody has the public key.

So how do you get the public key of the website you wish to communicate? In SSL, the certificate used for authentication also contains the public key of the website.

Message-->[Public Key]-->Encrypted Message-->[Private Key]-->Message

The most common use for SSL/TLS is in secure web connections using a client browser to connect to an SSL enabled web server. Therefore the client's web browser has SSL modules embedded that support the SSL/TLS technology. This makes using SSL/TLS virtually transparent to the client's end user which is a good thing as we want the web security to be as unobtrusive as possible. Hence the client's web browser does all the heavy lifting in the background and it is responsible for initiating the connection to the web-server and handling the SSL/TLS certificate transaction through what is known as an SSL/TLS handshake. During the initial handshake the web-server is challenged to authenticate its identity – after all the client wants to be sure they are communicating with the real server and not some fraud – and to achieve this the web-server sends the client a copy of its public digital certificate. Upon receiving the web-servers public certificate, which contains the public encryption key, the client's browser must then verify that the certificate and hence the keys are genuine. Once the browser is satisfied that the web-server is whom they claim to be then the handshake transaction will continue and a secure authenticated communications channel established.

However, in other use cases for SSL, for example in secure telnet, SSH, and PuTTY where there is no browser within the loop the SSL server will send the public key and then prompt the client to accept or decline the certificate. In other secure applications especially where there is no obvious way for client input such as using SSL to secure a MySQL connection then the servers public key will need to be physically exchanged and stored on the client prior to the secure connection being made. This is not really a problem as in most cases the SSL/TLS certificate being used is not for the public per se but for a private group of internal users so a self signed certificate is typically used and manually installed on each client.

What are the Different Types of SSL Certificate?

As of 2016 the market for digital certificates was controlled by three large Certificate Authorities. Almost 1/3 of all SSL certificates issued were by Symantec who were the largest CA with GoDaddy and Comodo following closely behind. Between them these three organizations account for more than ¾ of all SSL certificates issued.

However there is another angle to consider when we look at overall SSL certificate sales and that is which type of certificate is predominant? Certificate authorities typically sell certificates in three broad categories of assurance: *domain-validated* certificates simply validate control over a domain name; *organisation-validated* certificates include the strict verification of the identity of the organisation; and *Extended Validation* certificates, which increase the level of identity checking done to meet a recognised industry standard.

According to Netscape's SSL survey 2016 – 'Domain-validated certificates account for circa 70% of all certificates, EV accounts for fewer than 5%, with the remainder being organisation-validated. This overall split varies by certificate authorities, sometimes significantly — with some CAs, such as DigiCert and Verizon Business not offering domain-validated certificates at all. On the other hand the second biggest CA in terms of certificates issued is GoDaddy where almost all of its certificates are 'domain-validated'.

Not all SSL certificates are the same and some have more demanding prerequisites that others consequently there has arisen a number of different types of SSL certificates available on the market today that serves different purposes.

- Self-signed certificates are as the name implies generated internally and are usually not for authentication as much as for encryption. A self-signed certificate is generated by the businesses IT and is not issued by a third party CA. Since the website owners generate their own certificate, it is not as trusted as a fully authenticated and verified SSL certificate issued by a CA. Self-signed SSL certificates will always cause a browser to initiate a warning not to proceed unless the user explicitly instructs the browser to over-ride the security warning and accept the certificate. Alternatively the self-signed certificate can be manually installed into the client's browser but that isn't very scalable.

- A Domain Validated certificate may be considered an entry-level SSL certificate and as it verifies only the domain registration and ownership it can be issued quickly. No additional checks are carried out to ensure that the owner of the domain is a valid business entity.

- A fully authenticated SSL certificate is the first step to robust online security. A fully authenticated SSL certificate takes longer to issue, and is considerably more expensive. This is because the CA's verification process is more stringent as these certificates are issued only after the organization passes a number of validation procedures and checks. These verification steps will strive to confirm the existence of the business, the ownership of the domain, and the user's authority to apply for the certificate.

- Extended Validation (EV) SSL certificates offer the highest industry standard for authentication and provide the best level of customer trust available. When consumers visit a website secured with an EV SSL certificate, the address bar turns green (in high-security browsers) and a special field appears with the name of the legitimate website owner along with the name of the security provider that issued the EV SSL certificate. It also displays the name of the certificate holder and issuing CA in the address bar. This visual reassurance has helped increase consumer confidence in e-commerce.

- Wildcard Certificates are used to get round the problem of multiple sub domains on a server. A domain name is often used with a number of different host suffixes. So long as the domain remains the same, the SSL certificate will authenticate all sub domains that are attached to the registered domain. For example, *.example.com, example.com, www.example.com, mail.example.com, etc.

- A SAN (Subject Alternative Name) SSL certificate allows more than one domain to be added to a single SSL certificate. This is necessary in situation whereby two or more domains reside on the same physical web server and IP address for example in a service provider's web server, which may be supporting tens or hundreds of virtual machines.

In order to support SAN SSL there has to be a method for distinguishing which server (domain) is to be initially contacted during the SSL/TLS handshake therefore we use a technique called SNI or Server Name Indicator.

Server Name Indication

SNI stands for Server Name Indication and is an extension of the TLS protocol. The purpose of the SNI method is to indicate which hostname is being contacted by the browser at the beginning of the 'handshake'-process as many hosts could well co-habit a server.

SNI allows a server to multi-tenant websites and present multiple certificates on the same IP address and TCP port number. This is preferred to having multiple secure websites being served by a wildcard certificate.

Instead SNI facilitates that multi tenant secure web sites running off the same IP address no longer require those sites to use the same certificate instead they can have their own domain certificate.

The issue was that when making a TLS connection the client requests a digital certificate from the web server. Once the server sends it own certificate, the client examines it and compares the name it was trying to connect to with the name included in the certificate.

If a match occurs the connection proceeds as normal but as is likely to happen in a multi-tenant scenario and a match is not found the user may be warned of the discrepancy and the connection may abort as the mismatch indicates suspicious behavior akin to an attempted man-in-the-middle attack.

Server Name Indication (SNI) is the solution to this problem.

Browsers that support SNI will instead send the name to the name of the website the visitor wants to connect with during the initialization of the secured connection, so that the server knows which certificate to send back.

SNI can be troublesome as some older browsers/systems cannot support the technique however this is now a rarity. This is because the SSL/TLS library can be transmitted as part of the request and as part of the operating system.

The first step of course after deciding on which certificate best suits your requirement is to install OpenSSL or another SSL module onto your server, if it isn't already installed, and then create a CSR (a certificate request) This is not difficult but does cause some confusion, as the server must have OpenSSL or some other SSL application installed; therefore, the steps to installing an OpenSSL package for Apache are listed below in the next section.

Installing OpenSSL

OpenSSL is the most popular SSL/TLS package and is open source so is freely available. OpenSSL is based on the excellent SSLeay library developed by Eric Young and Tim Hudson. The OpenSSL toolkit is an Apache-style license, which means that you are free to get and use it for commercial and non-commercial purposes subject to some simple license conditions.

You can download OpenSSL here:

https://www.openssl.org/source/

At the time of writing (May 2015) the latest OpenSSL version is:

The latest stable version is the 1.1.0 series of releases. Also available is the 1.0.2 series. This is also our Long Term Support (LTS) version (support will be provided until 31st December 2019). The 0.9.8, 1.0.0 and 1.0.1 versions are now out of support and should not be used.

5080   2017-Feb-16 12:03:39   openssl-1.1.0e.tar.gz (SHA256) (PGP sign) (SHA1)

OpenSSL though is typically installed in most Linux versions repositories if not already preinstalled. However if it is not then here is an example of how to compile, install and configure for Ubuntu.

1. Download OpenSSL

wget http://www.openssl.org/source/openssl-1.0.2a.tar.gz

2. Extract files

tar -xvzf openssl-1.0.2a.tar.gz

3. Change dir

cd openssl-1.0.2a

4. Configure OpenSSL

./config --prefix=/usr/local/openssl --openssldir=/usr/local/openssl –libdir=lib

5. Install

make install

6. Test the version

/usr/local/openssl/bin/openssl version

**Note – version openssl-1.0.2a now requires a patch, so download the patch before installation

```
patch -Np1 -i ../openssl-1.0.2a-fix_parallel_build-2.patch &&

./config --prefix=/usr/local/ssl       \
     --openssldir=/usr/local/ssl \
     --libdir=lib         \
     shared            \
     zlib-dynamic &&
make
```

Config Commands

shared: This parameter forces the creation of shared libraries along with the static libraries.

zlib-dynamic: This parameter adds compression/decompression functionality using the libz library.

Now that OpenSSL is installed on our server, we can start to use it to create our CSR.

How do you create a SSL Certificate request?

Each CA will have their individual instructions but they follow the same general procedure:

To create an SSL certificate, you need to start with a certificate request (or, as some certificate authorities like to put it, "certificate signing request", since that's exactly what they are doing, in so much as you provide the server name, IP, domain, company name etc and turn that into a small piece of code that you send them. The CA will then verify the details, then sign it and give you the result back, again as a small piece of code, thus making it authentic according to their policies).

The first step, when obtaining the SSL certificate, is to fill out the certificate authority's application form and that will require generating and then cutting and pasting an SSL CSR to the form.

An example of how to raise an SSL request on a web server running Linux and OpenSSL is:

To create the SSL certificate request, which is just a small piece of code generated on a server running OpenSSL we have to follow a CSR request process. For convenience and to keep the private keys secure we will generate the CSR on the web server that the certificate will be deployed. This is extremely important, as it will use the domain name of the server or the host name as it is known to clients in DNS to make up the SSL certificate request. Private IP addresses are no longer supported as a means of identifying a host certificate as previously was the case and those previously issued were revoked as of October 2016.

Should I create the CSR on the machine that will host the Certificate?

Wherever possible it is best to create the certificate on the machine on which it will be served. It is not a necessity by any means as the certificate can be used on any machine that resolves through DNS to the FQDN domain name that is on the certificate or to the Public Address if that is what you plan to use for the certificate. Either way the Domain name or the IP Address will need to resolve to your name and contact details via a 'Whois Lookup' as that is how the CA is likely to verify the domain/IP owner. The reason though that it is best to create the CSR on the machine the certificate will be served from is that during the process of creating the CSR OpenSSL also creates the cert.key which is the private key that will be associated with the SSL certificate. Therefore creating the secret key directly onto the server where it will reside is optimum as it means you do not have to copy it and move it to another server. Indeed on Windows servers you will have to first install the certificate onto the same machine that you created the CSR on as that is where the private key resides. Then you will have to do a backup and export of the certificate and the private key before importing into the machine on which it is designated to run on. On Linux machines you can just copy the certificate and the private keys from the server you created the CSR and private key onto the designated server but remember the private key is precious and you do not want copies of it on memory sticks or on people's laptops.

In short unless there is a very good reason for not creating the CSR on the designated server where the certificate will be served always take this option at the very least it will be far tidier and way more secure.

So now we are ready to go here is an example for creating an OpenSSL CSR for an Apache web server:

1. Login to your server via your terminal client (ssh). At the prompt, type:

```
openssl req -new -newkey rsa:2048 -nodes -keyout server.key -out
server.csr
```

   (where server is the name of your server)

2. This begins the process of generating two files: the **Private-Key** file for the decryption of your SSL Certificate, and a certificate signing request (**CSR**) file (used to apply for your SSL Certificate) with apache openssl.

3. When you are prompted for the Common Name (domain name), enter the fully qualified domain name for the site you are securing. For example: If you intend to secure the URL https://www.yourdomain.com, then your CSR's common name must be www.yourdomain.com.

   If you are generating an Apache CSR for a Wildcard SSL Certificate your common name should start with an asterisk (such as *.example.com). You will then be prompted for your organizational information, beginning with geographic information. For example the country code is the 2 letter ISO abbreviation such as US or UK. Importantly the Organization Name MUST be the exact legal name of your organization. Do not abbreviate your organization name. There may be default information set already.

This will then create your openssl .csr file.

Verify that the CSR file has been created OK.

```
openssl req -noout -text -in ~/server.com.ssl/server.com.csr
```

4. Open the CSR file with a text editor and copy and paste it (including the BEGIN and END tags) into the CA's Certificate order form supplied by the CA.

Save (backup) the generated .key file as it will be required later for Certificate installation.

Copy the .csr file and paste it into the CA application form.

Note

Google have recently announced that they are going to start reporting that SSL certificates that are signed with a SHA-1 Hash will be treated as having a lower security than those signed with newer, higher strength hashes such as SHA-256 or SHA-512.

So if that is of concern follow the steps below:

1. Generate a SSL Key File

Firstly, you will need to generate a key file. The example below will generate a 2048-bit key file with a SHA-256 signature.

```
openssl genrsa -out key_name.key 2048
```

If you want extra security, you could increase the bit lengths.

```
openssl genrsa -out key_name.key 4096
```

** Please, note that both these examples will not add a password to the key file. To do that you will need to add -des3 to the command. However, if you add a password you will have to be there to type it in every time the server reboots, or worse the web server is restarted – not a good idea! However, it is also vital if you do not password protect the private key that you secure it!

*** Please also make sure that you remember where you store this key file as it will be needed when you upload the SSL/TLS certificate that you receive from the CA with your public/private key pair.

2. Create a Certificate Signing Request (CSR)

This step will create the actually request file that you will submit to the Certificate Authority (CA) of your choice.

```
openssl req -out CSR.csr -key key_name.key -new -sha256
```

You can check that your Certificate Signing Request (CSR) has the correct signature by running the following.

```
openssl req -in CSR.csr -noout -text
```

It should display the following if the signature is correct.

Signature Algorithm: sha256WithRSAEncryption

The certificate authority performs various checks (according to their policies) and usually waits for payment from you. Once that is complete, they send you the new SSL certificate.

How to install the SSL certificate

Now that you have received the SSL/TLS certificate from the issuing Certificate Authority (CA) it will need to be installed onto your web-server. This should not be a difficult task if you follow the instructions provided by your hosted web-server provider. However if you have a self hosted server then you need to install the certificate yourself and the procedure is dependent on several factors such as where you installed SSL, your web server and the location of the CSR key file – which was created when you created the certificate request.

Installing the SSL Certificate on IIS

For example, to install an SSL certificate on Windows IIS the procedure is pretty intuitive only some of the terminology can be confusing.

To start the upload the SSL Certificate process then go to the Start menu, go to **Administrative Tools**, and click on **Internet Information Services (IIS) Manager**.

Then Click on the name of the server in the Connections column on the left. Double-click on **Server Certificates**.

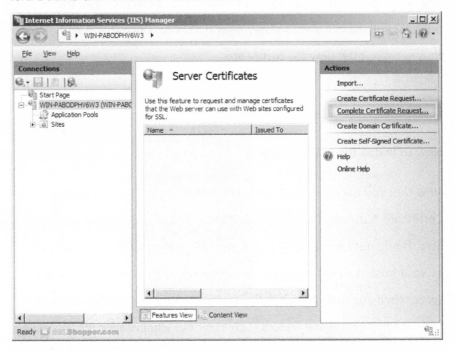

Figure 1-2

Click the button with the three dots and select the server certificate that you received from the certificate authority. If the certificate doesn't have a .cer file extension, select to view all types. Enter any friendly name you want so you can keep track of the certificate on this server. Click **OK**.

If successful, you will see your newly installed certificate in the list. If you receive an error stating that the request or private key cannot be found, make sure you are using the correct certificate and that you are installing it to the same server that you generated the CSR on. If you are sure of those two things, you may just need to create a new Certificate Request and reissue/replace the certificate. Contact your certificate authority if you have problems with this.

If everything has gone OK then all that is not required is to bind the certificate to a website and to do that is straightforward. To do this you need to navigate to the Start Page -> Server -> Sites (default web site) and expand the sites folder and click on the website that you want to bind the certificate to.

Click on **Bindings...**in the right column.

Change the Type to **https** and then select the SSL certificate that you just installed. Click **OK**.

Figure 1-3

And that is all there is to it.

Installing the SSL Cert on Apache

On the other hand with Apache or Tomcat on a locally hosted server we will need to do a lot of the configuration manually but so long as you have installed OpenSSL and Apache/Tomcat to the default locations the SSL certificate installation should be relatively straightforward.

The first thing you need to do is check the installation directories for OpenSSL and Apache they should be located in a directory path similar to this: /usr/local/ssl and /usr/local/apache2 (or sometimes httpd) respectively.

The key point here is that you need to know the exact paths for configuring the Apache conf file for SSL and where it can locate the SSL key files.

Therefore when we receive the SSL cert from the CA we first need to check it is valid by running the command in SSL:

```
openssl verify -CAfile /path/to/trusted_ca.crt -purpose sslserver
server.crt
```

Next, check that the output of these two commands is the same, i.e., that the certificate corresponds to the private key:

```
openssl x509 -noout -modulus -in server.pem | openssl sha1
openssl rsa -noout -modulus -in server.key | openssl sha1
```

Now install your key (generated as server.key above) and certificate (server.crt), into /etc/apache2/ssl, or your preferred Apache2 config directory, if that's different. As mentioned above, it's important to make sure that the server.key is readable only by root, while the server certificate should be world-readable, but owned and writeable only by root.

Next we need to make changes to the Apache configuration file and we do this by editing the following:

```
/etc/apache2/apache2.conf directly to include the lines:

Listen 80

Listen 443
```

Next, edit /etc/apache2/sites-enabled/yoursite to use the SSL settings. Separating the regular and secure server settings out by using VirtualHosts is the easiest option in terms of maintainability. Any configuration outside the VirtualHosts sections (such as setting the ServerAdmin) will apply to both (and any other) VirtualHosts. Add the following section to your config file:

```
# ==================================================
# SSL/TLS settings
# ==================================================
NameVirtualHost *:443


<VirtualHost *:443>
```

```
DocumentRoot "/local/www/ssl_html"

SSLEngine on
SSLOptions +StrictRequire

<Directory />
  SSLRequireSSL
</Directory>

SSLProtocol -all +TLSv1 +SSLv3
SSLCipherSuite HIGH:MEDIUM:!aNULL:+SHA1:+MD5:+HIGH:+MEDIUM

SSLRandomSeed startup file:/dev/urandom 1024
SSLRandomSeed connect file:/dev/urandom 1024

SSLSessionCache shm:/usr/local/apache2/logs/ssl_cache_shm
SSLSessionCacheTimeout 600

SSLCertificateFile /etc/apache2/ssl/server.crt
SSLCertificateKeyFile /etc/apache2/ssl/server.key

SSLVerifyClient none
SSLProxyEngine off

<IfModule mime.c>
  AddType application/x-x509-ca-cert     .crt
```

```
    AddType application/x-pkcs7-crl        .crl
  </IfModule>


  SetEnvIf User-Agent ".*MSIE.*" \
    nokeepalive ssl-unclean-shutdown \
    downgrade-1.0 force-response-1.0
</VirtualHost>
```

- SSLEngine must be enabled so that the server uses SSL.

- DocumentRoot sets the root directory for this virtual host. This means that you can separate secure content entirely from regular content.

- SSLRequireSSL requires SSL to be used (on this virtual host): i.e., a user can't connect to this host using a regular HTTP request. This is why we separate out the secure and regular root directory.

- SSLProtocol disables all protocols other than TLS v1.0 and SSL v3.0. This will be OK for current web browsers.

- SSLCipherSuite is set to use only HIGH and MEDIUM security cipher suites. SHA1 is considered to be more secure than MD5 so is preferred.

- SSLCertificateFile and SSLCertificateKeyFile should be set to the locations where you put your certificate and key files.

- SSLVerifyClient should be set to none if not using client authentication.

To run the regular server on port 80, add the following section to the config file:

```
NameVirtualHost *:80

<VirtualHost *:80>
    DocumentRoot "/local/www/html"
    # Host-specific directory setup, options, etc
    # Most of these options are likely to be set outside the VirtualHosts
    # sections.
</VirtualHost>
```

After you've saved the edited configuration file, restart the web server. If you did use a passphrase when generating your certificate, you'll need to enter it when challenged.

Installing SSL Certificate on Nginx

We first create our CSR file using OpenSSL as already described under the /etc/ssl directory and while we wait the certificate from the CA we can start to modify our Nginx configuration to be able to use them.

In order to do this we will need to make some adjustments to our configuration to support SSL/TLS and also to make some detailed configurations adjustments to the default SSL modules.

1. First we need to create a configuration snippet containing our SSL key and certificate file locations.

2. For this we will create a configuration snippet, which contains some strong SSL settings that we can use with certificates in the future.

3. Then we will adjust our Nginx server blocks to handle SSL requests and use the two snippets above.

4. We will copy our SSL certificates received from the CA to the secure key storage locations

The reason we use this method of configuring is so that we keep Nginx server blocks clean by putting common configuration segments into reusable modules.

Create a Configuration Snippet Pointing to the SSL Key and Certificate

First, let's create a new Nginx configuration snippet in the /etc/nginx/snippets directory.

To properly distinguish the purpose of this file, let's call it ssl-certs.conf:

```
sudo nano /etc/nginx/snippets/ssl-certs.conf
```

Within this file, we just need to set the ssl_certificate directive to our certificate file and the ssl_certificate_key to the associated key. In our case, this will look like this:

```
/etc/nginx/snippets/ssl-certs.conf
ssl_certificate /etc/ssl/certs/your_domain_name.crt;
ssl_certificate_key /etc/ssl/private/your_domain_name.key;
```

The server certificate is a public entity. It is sent to every client that connects to the server. The private key is a secure entity and should be stored in a file with restricted access, however, it must be readable by nginx's master process. The private key may alternately be stored in the same file as the certificate:

```
ssl_certificate /etc/ssl/your_domain_name.cert;
ssl_certificate_key /etc/ssl/your_domain_name.cert;
```

in this case the file access rights should also be restricted. Although the certificate and the key are stored in one file, only the certificate is sent to a client

When you've added those lines, save and close the file.

Create a Configuration Snippet with Strong Encryption Settings

Next, we will create another snippet that will define some SSL settings. This will set Nginx up with a strong SSL cipher suite and enable some advanced features that will help keep our server secure.

The parameters we will set can be reused in future Nginx configurations, so we will give the file a generic name:

```
sudo nano /etc/nginx/snippets/ssl-params.conf
```

To set up Nginx SSL securely, we will be using a modern choice of ciphers that are suited to supporting all popular browsers and web applications. Unfortunately, choosing a cipher-suite is not a black and white decision as there can be many trade-offs and compromises required between being highly secure on one hand and on the other capable of widely supporting older browsers and business apps. For example it is easy to say well I will only support the latest TLS v1.2 and disable all SSL and earlier TLS versions as they have vulnerabilities only to discover that older browsers or devices using Android 4 OS cannot connect to your server.

The choice of which config you use will depend largely on what you need to support. Later in the section on SSL cipher-suites we will examine these options in detail but for now we will use a popular cipher-suite that will provide great security and support all modern web browsers.

```
/etc/nginx/snippets/ssl-params.conf
```

```
ssl_protocols TLSv1 TLSv1.1 TLSv1.2;

ssl_prefer_server_ciphers on;

ssl_ciphers

"EECDH+AESGCM:EDH+AESGCM:AES256+EECDH:AES256+EDH";

ssl_ecdh_curve secp384r1;

ssl_session_cache shared:SSL:10m;

ssl_session_tickets off;

ssl_stapling on;

ssl_stapling_verify on;

resolver 8.8.8.8 8.8.4.4 valid=300s;

resolver_timeout 5s;

add_header Strict-Transport-Security "max-age=63072000;

includeSubdomains";

add_header X-Frame-Options DENY;

add_header X-Content-Type-Options nosniff;
```

Save and close the file when you are finished.

Adjust the Nginx Configuration to Use SSL

Now that we have our snippets, we can adjust our Nginx configuration to enable SSL.

We will assume in this guide that you are using the default server block file in the /etc/nginx/sites-available directory. If you are using a different server block file, substitute its name in the below commands.

Before we go any further, let's back up our current server block file:

```
sudo cp /etc/nginx/sites-available/default /etc/nginx/sites-
available/default.bak
```

Now, open the server block file to make adjustments:

```
sudo nano /etc/nginx/sites-available/default
```

Inside, your server block probably begins like this:

```
/etc/nginx/sites-available/default
server {
    listen 80 default_server;
    listen [::]:80 default_server;

    # SSL configuration

    # listen 443 ssl default_server;
    # listen [::]:443 ssl default_server;


    . . .
```

We will be modifying this configuration so that unencrypted HTTP requests are automatically redirected to encrypted HTTPS. This offers the best security for our sites. However should you need to support both HTTP and HTTPS traffic, which is not advisable and against best practices, but is often a real world requirement then use the alternative configuration that follows the SSL only configuration at the end.

```
/etc/nginx/sites-available/default
server {
    listen 80 default_server;
    listen [::]:80 default_server;
    server_name server_domain_or_IP;
    return 301 https://$server_name$request_uri;
}
    # SSL configuration
  # listen 443 ssl default_server;
  # listen [::]:443 ssl default_server;
```

Next, we need to start a new server block directly below to contain the remaining configuration. We can uncomment the two listen directives that use port 443. We can add http2 to these lines in order to enable HTTP/2 within this block. Afterwards, we just need to include the two snippet files we set up:

Note: You may only have **one** listen directive that includes the default_server modifier for each IP version and port combination. If you have other server blocks enabled for these ports that have default_server set, you must remove the modifier from one of the blocks.

```
/etc/nginx/sites-available/default
server {
    listen 80 default_server;
    listen [::]:80 default_server;
    server_name server_domain_or_IP;
    return 301 https://$server_name$request_uri;
}

server {

    # SSL configuration

    listen 443 ssl http2 default_server;
    listen [::]:443 ssl http2 default_server;
    include snippets/ssl-certs.conf;
    include snippets/ssl-params.conf;


    . . .
```

Save and close the file when you are finished.

Configure for both HTTP and HTTPS Traffic

If you need to configure the web server to allow both encrypted and unencrypted content, you will have to configure Nginx a bit differently. This is generally not recommended as it is best to keep all HTTP and HTTPS traffic seperate, but in some situations it may be necessary. In this case, we have to allow traffic for both listening ports on 80 and 443 so we in effect just compress the two separate server blocks together and remove the redirect:

```
/etc/nginx/sites-available/default
server {
    listen 80 default_server;
    listen [::]:80 default_server;
    listen 443 ssl http2 default_server;
    listen [::]:443 ssl http2 default_server;

    server_name server_domain_or_IP;
    include snippets/ssl-certs.conf;
    include snippets/ssl-params.conf;

    . . .
```

Save and close the file when you are finished.

Installing the NGinx SSL Certificates

Nginx Server SSL Certificate Installation

1. Primary certificate and intermediate certificate.

   You should have received a **your_domain_name.pem** file from the CA in an email when your certificate was issued. This .pem file contains both your primary certificate and the intermediate certificate. If you have that .pem file you can skip to step 4.

   If you still need to concatenate your primary certificate and your intermediate certificate in to a single file, start with step 2.

2. Copy the Certificate files to your server.

   If you have received an Intermediate (.crt) and Primary Certificates (your_domain_name.crt). Copy them, along with the .key file you generated when you created the CSR, to the directory on your server where you will keep your certificate and key files. Make them readable only by root to increase security.

3. Concatenate the primary certificate and intermediate certificate.

   You need to concatenate the primary certificate file (your_domain_name.crt) and the intermediate certificate file (YourCA.crt) into a single pem file by running the following command:

```
cat your_domain_name.crt  YourCA.crt >> bundle.crt
```

   It is important to make sure the primary certificate is first and is followed by the intermediary cert if not you will get an error;

If the server certificate and the bundle have been concatenated in the wrong order,nginx will fail to start and will display the error message:

```
SSL_CTX_use_PrivateKey_file(" ... /www.example.com.key") failed
        (SSL: error:0B080074:x509 certificate routines:
        X509_check_private_key:key values mismatch)
```

This is because nginx has tried to use the private key with the bundle's first certificate instead of the server certificate.

4. Edit the Nginx virtual hosts file.

Now open your Nginx virtual host file for the website you are securing. If you need your site to be accessible through both secure (https) and non-secure (http) connections, you will need a server module for each type of connection. Make a copy of the existing non-secure server module and paste it below the original. Then add the lines in bold below:

```
server {

listen   443;

ssl   on;
ssl_certificate   /etc/ssl/your_domain_name.pem; (or bundle.crt)
ssl_certificate_key   /etc/ssl/your_domain_name.key;
```

```
server_name your.domain.com;

access_log /var/log/nginx/nginx.vhost.access.log;

error_log /var/log/nginx/nginx.vhost.error.log;

location / {

root   /home/www/public_html/your.domain.com/public/;

index  index.html;

}


}
```

Adjust the file names to match your certificate files:

- **ssl_certificate** should be your primary certificate combined with the intermediate certificate that you made in the previous step (e.g. your_domain_name.crt).

- **ssl_certificate_key** should be the key file generated when you created the CSR.

Restart Nginx.

Run the following command to restart Nginx:

```
sudo /etc/init.d/nginx restart
```

What does an SSL Certificate contain?

So now that we have generated and installed our SSL certificate we can start to use it to authenticate our server as well as encrypt traffic flowing between a client browser and our website. However, what is on this certificate and how does it both authenticate our server and encrypt the traffic.

An SSL certificate holds verified information regarding:

- Who owns the certificate

- How long the certificate is valid and a unique identifier

- The owner's public key

- The CA's signature that is certifying the certificate

This system works well if everyone trusts the Certificate Authorities, but when they don't or if there is an issue the system has a tendency to fail. Consequently, if using SSL certificates it is paramount that you use one of the major trusted authorities, because with SSL certificates you definitely get what you pay for. Cheap and cheerful SSL certificates are available some are even free, but many will not be recognized by standard browsers, or come with no support whatsoever. However as this is our default system of authentication and encryption over the Internet, we have to make do with it until something better comes along.

An SSL Certificate verifies who you are.

The major point about SSL or TLS is that it definitely verifies that you are who you claim to be. This is hugely important when dealing with secure internet sites such as email or internet banking. What an SSL certificate issued by a trusted CA can do is provide confidence and trust to clients and customers. Furthermore, a genuine SSL certificate does not just verify that the server – with whom you as a client are communicating with - is the genuine entity but that all communications between each party is secured by encryption, thereby securing the privacy and integrity of the conversation.

This is the primary use for SSL/TLS the ability to authenticate the server so that web users know who they are talking too. For example, with web banking a customer must be sure that the server in the internet, lurking somewhere in the cloud belongs to their bank and not some group of hackers. Similarly, once that server's authenticity has been verified the customer will want their transaction to be private hence the need for strong encryption. SSL provided that reassurance and confidence, which enables financial web transactions to take place, it is also the bedrock of all ecommerce, online government and healthcare websites that handle private personal information. However, SSL/TLS despite its vast importance has grown that fast due to the explosive demand of the internet that verification checks are not perhaps all that they should be – and this has weakened the reputation of SSL.

Ok, so how do they share keys privately?

The genius of SSL and all other symmetric/asymmetrical key algorithms comes down to how two parties can exchange encryption keys securely over an unsecure medium, for example the internet with complete privacy even from an eavesdropper viewing the handshake.

SSL combines both symmetric and asymmetric encryption. Symmetric encryption is achieved using a shared key between the website and the browser which is created at session initiation. Asymmetric encryption is achieved by using a pair of matching keys, known as the "private key", or "server key" and the "Public key", or "Certificate". While asymmetric encryption removes the burden of exchanging keys, it is consuming a great amount of CPU resources. In a "best of both worlds" approach, SSL will use an asymmetric key pair during the connection phase, known as the "SSL handshake", during which the website and browser will exchange a unique generated key used to symmetrically encrypt the rest of the connection.

The SSL handshake is a process in which an SSL connection is established. To do so, the server must offer a valid certificate confirming the identity of the website and both client and server need to find compatible cipher suites and compression methods.

The way it works is that, the client's browser asks for an SSL protected page from the web server. The server responds with an x509 (SSL) certificate (signed public key) and a set of intermediate certificates needed for confirmation of the site identity.

The client's browser then must validate the website's certificate (public key) and sends in response a random key encrypted with the web server's public key.

The web server upon receiving this response can decrypt and retrieve the client's random key. Therefore, both the website and browser have a shared random key to use for symmetric encryption. The reason being is that the symmetric key is a couple of order of magnitudes faster than using the public/private key pair for asymmetric encryption and results in similar sized savings in CPU overhead.

This is the foundation for Secure Socket Layer (SSL) encryption, which is a secure internet connection widely used by many internet protocol, especially web traffic. While an application, such as a browser, can treat an SSL connection like any other connection, sophisticated algorithms are used to validate the identity of the web servers and encrypt the transmissions whilst maintain the secure tunnel for the duration of the session.

Certificate Chains

As we saw earlier SSL certificates, have many properties associated with them apart from their feature of being a public key. Each certificate has a subject, which it "certifies", such as a domain, or a signing service provided by an authority. It also contains an issuer, and the name of a certificate that "signed" this certificate. Originally back in the 90's there were only a few highly reputable organization that were allowed to be Certificate Authorities as the whole system relies on their diligence, integrity and dependability. However, having a few root CA's manage the entire internet proved to be unsustainable, so other organizations verified by the root CA's were enlisted to help meet the demand for SSL certificates. Today there are hundreds of such CA organizations forming a hierarchal tree structure with each branch verified by the one preceding it until we reach the root CAs. Therefore, each CA at one level effectively verifies the certificates of CAs at a lower level and when a number of certificates sign each other in this hierarchal order, a "certificate chain" is formed.

The significance of the certification chain is that every browser will then need to have a package of bundled certificates, root and common intermediate certificates of trusted certificate authorities preinstalled or hardcoded. Consequently, for SSL to work the websites public key, or an intermediate key that signed the websites key, has to be present in the browser's bundle of root, and intermediate keys. If a certificate that is present in the browser's bundle of certificates has signed the website's certificate, the chain of certificates is considered authentic, and thus the identity of the web site is confirmed.

Root Certificate authorities, CA, for short, are organizations that have their root certificates bundled with all the major browser products and thus all the certificates signed by their root certificates are considered valid. Therefore, a hierarchy forms were those root CAs will validate the identity of other CAs and they will in turn sign certificates for a further layer of CAs and so on. Of course this means that each certificate must come with all the intermediate CA signed certificates bundled with it. Furthermore, the web server will have to pass this bundle of certificates to the browser as without them the browser might not be able to verify the chain back to the root CA.

An example of a certificate chain:

Certificate chain:
First certificate in chain - my website's certificate
    Certificate subject: www.mywebsite.com
    Issuer: Some CA, product of class X
Signed by:
Second certificate in chain - intermediate certificate
    Certificate subject: Some CA, product of class X
    Issuer: Some CA root
Signed by:
Third certificate in chain - Root certificate of a CA, self-signed
    Certificate subject: Some CA root
    Issuer: Some CA root

An interesting point here is that this hierarchy is not to share the burden of online verification requests similar say to the way a credit card authentication and transaction verification request is performed. It is simply to relieve the burden of issuing, signing and revoking certificates as no online, real-time verification of a web server's public certificate actually takes place. Instead, what happens is that the client's browser that is verifying the server certificate simply checks the public certificate vault and if they have the corresponding signed certificate of the CA then the web server's identity is validated. Browsers do not go out of their way to validate certificates online if they can possibly avoid it – and as we will see this can lead to issues.

Certification Renewal and Revocation

The principle behind SSL/TLS of exchanging Public and Private asymmetric keys is sound in theory and has stood the test of time in practice – there can be no more onerous environment than the internet. Issuing a certificate and even diligently verifying a requesting company or domain owner for an SSL certificate is only part of the task. A much bigger issue is what to do when things go wrong.

Things can go very wrong with SSL certificates from simple mistakes when the certificate is requested, and issued through to lost or stolen certificates and keys. Therefore there has to be a way to manage such events and that requires a process to renew and revoke certificates.

SSL certificates are issued with an explicit life span that is encoded into the digital certificate telling the world its start and expiry date. Therefore to be accepted and verified by the browser the date must fall between the two boundaries. This incidentally is why you can get so many issues when client browsers are not running internet synchronized time as a variance of even ten or so minutes can cause the handshake to fail because timing is critical to the process of verification of the certificate. However, there are good reasons other than repeat fees that dictate why a certificate must be regularly renewed and these are due to loss, theft or fraud.

The problem with a digital certificate is that if you lose it you can no longer securely authenticate your web servers or accept SSL inbound connections – you can but it would not be safe or ethical -until you can get a new certificate issued. Therefore it is critical that the certificate and SSL keys are backed up and securely stored. An even worse situation is if the SSL keys are somehow misappropriated because how they are as good as useless. This is simply because their only value is that in your possession they prove your identity, but if someone else also has them or they are publicly available on the internet then anyone can use them and claim to be you. Now of course, they would need to use the same domain name that is on the certificate and poison the DNS to reflect the new IP address so that traffic was diverted to the new fraud server but other than that it would work as it is just another MITM attack. Now that is very bad news but what is far worse is that you will be doomed forever unless there is a way to revoke that stolen certificate.

Revoking certificates works in two ways, the official way which is:

Certificate Revocation List (CRL)

That CAs should revoke compromised certificates and duly add them to a Certificate Revocation List (CRL) which it will duly publish browsers will then download the CRLs and check that a certificate undergoing the validation process is not on that list. There are of course several issues with this model that made it redundant pretty quickly. Firstly, this is the internet and the numbers of revoked certificates is vast and browsers are not going to want to keep downloading this huge list every time a CA – and there are hundreds of them – publish a new CRL. Secondly, theoretically all associated certificates, i.e. the intermediaries should be also checked for revocation, but this would cause much delay due to recursive lookups and result in unacceptable latency. The result was that few browsers – remember this was also back in the days of limited and expensive bandwidth – refused to comply and simply failed to download let alone check any CRL. Subsequently, the smaller and then larger CAs stopped producing CRLs because no-one was using them.

Online Certificate Status Protocol (OCSP)

An alternative was to use a system called Online Certificate Status Protocol (OCSP), which is an Internet protocol used for obtaining the revocation status of an X.509 digital certificate. OCSP overcomes the chief limitation of CRL: the fact that large updates must be frequently downloaded and parsed to keep the list current at the client end. The way OCSP works is when a user attempts to access an SSL server; OCSP sends a request for certificate status information to an OCSP server (responder) on the internet, which is typically run by a CA. The OCSP responder sends back a signed response of "current", "expired," or "unknown." Furthermore, OCSP can support more than one level of CA so it can check intermediaries within certificate chains. It can do this because OCSP requests may be chained between peer responders to query the issuing CA appropriate for the subject certificate, with responders validating each other's responses against the root CA using their own OCSP requests.

OCSP has obvious advantages over CRL which is all but obsolete but it does still have issues of its own. Firstly, OCSP is only marginally effective against the worst case scenario of stolen SSL keys as any MiTM attacker worth their salt would see the outbound OCSP request and simply block the reply. This is because browsers still failover to allowing the SSL connection in the case of a timed out response from an OCSP responder. That might seem to be counter-productive but browser vendors are far more interested in their products and their customers experience than whether an X.509 certificate is valid or not. Secondly, the CA responders bare a heavy burden handling OCSP requests from every client on the internet wanting to connect to one of their customer's high-traffic SSL certificated servers. Consequently there will be latency and delays during peak times due to congestion caused by the enormous traffic flows through the responders. Thirdly, OCSP checking potentially impairs users' privacy and slows down browsing, since it requires the client to contact a third party (the CA) to confirm the validity of each certificate that it encounters.

Moreover, there is again the issue that if the client fails to connect or receive a response from the OCSP responder, then it is forced to decide between two options, neither of which is desirable. The client may choose to continue the connection anyway, which is typically what happens and that is defeating the purpose of OCSP revocation checking. On the other hand it may choose to terminate the connection based on the principle that if the certificate cannot be validated then it cannot be trusted, which decreases usability and could result in excessive loss of business for the CA's customers.

OCSP - Stapling

In order to resolve the issue whereby the client browser effectively bore the burden of authenticating the web server certificate a method called TLS Service Status Request or more commonly as OCSP stapling was devised. With this extension to OCSP it was the responsibility of the server or the party holding and presenting the SSL certificate to contact the OCSP responder. They would then request a signed time-stamped validation of their certificate status, which it would then append to its SSL certificate during the standard SSL handshake.

OCSP stapling resolves many of the base OCSP protocols problems such as heavy unsupportable traffic from clients. As now only the certificate presenters the domain holders request validation from the CAs at regular intervals and not on every connection. Similarly, OCSP-stapling has moved the brunt of the resource burden back onto the certificate holder. It also means that the client software no longer needs to disclose users' browsing habits to any third party i.e. the CA.

So that is how revoked certificates should be handled but the real issue and it is a bit of a revelation is that certification revocation has no place in SSL as the protocol only specifies how and when a certificate should be exchanged. The certificate itself is not a requirement in SSL specifications. Indeed, the SSL specification does not describe certificate validation; for that, you must look at the specification for X.509 digital certificates, in which you will see that it is a much more complex process than what is commonly believed to be the case.

The interesting part is that SSL doesn't have a part to play in SSL certificate verification and hence has nothing to say regards checking of the revocation status as that process is part of certificate validation. However X.509, the certificate specification does have views on how X.509 certificate life cycles are managed. With regards revocation, it seems the client is actually free to do it in any way it sees fit and many browser vendors choose to take them at their word – so they do nothing at all.

In the X.509 specifications, revocation status can be ascertained by downloading and validating CRL (Certificate Revocation Lists) or obtaining OCSP responses from OCSP responders. Theoretically, revocation status should be obtained for all certificates, i.e. the server certificate but also the intermediate CA certificates used to validate the server certificates, and all other certificates used to validate CRL and OCSP responses (this can become highly recursive). The aggregate cost (especially in download time) can become prohibitive, which is why many clients rely on a weaker but faster model (e.g. checking status only for the server certificate itself, not the intermediate CA; or checking no status at all).

How does SSL Handshake work?

The Secure Socket Layer protocol uses the SSL Handshake authenticate the website and to set up the encryption that will be used later in the session, I.E when the user may login. This is in short how it works.

1. A browser requests a secure page on a website (usually https://).

2. The web server responds and sends its public key as part of its certificate.

3. The browser checks that the certificate is valid and was issued by a trusted party (usually a trusted root CA or an intermediate in a valid certificate), that the certificate is still valid and that the certificate is related to the site visited.

4. The browser then uses the public key part of the certificate, to encrypt a random symmetric encryption key and sends it to the

server with the encrypted URL required as well as other encrypted http data.

5. The web server decrypts the symmetric encryption key using its private key and uses the symmetric key to decrypt the URL and http data.

6. The web server sends back the requested html document and http data encrypted with the symmetric key.

7. The browser decrypts the http data and html document using the symmetric key and displays the information.

That is the simplified version and is all that is generally required to know, however a more detailed explanation of the message exchanges (handshake) is included below.

The user's browser (client) and web application (server) establish an SSL handshake that begins a secure connection through the exchange of messages. The procedure to establish an SSL handshake is to exchange the following messages:

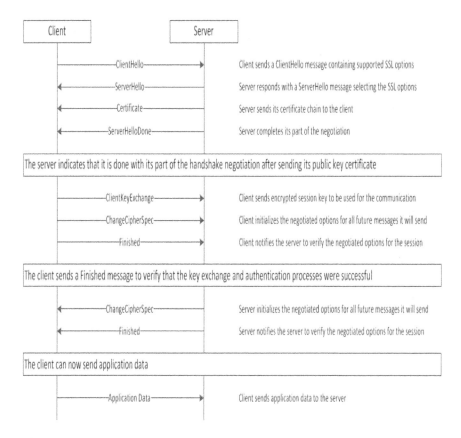

Figure 1-4

The SSL messages determine the parameters of the encrypted communication channel that the two parties will use. It is important that the client and server agree on the message details, such as the protocol version, cipher suites, secure renegotiation, or client certificate requests. Otherwise the handshake will fail. The SSL handshake has the following messaging components:

ClientHello

When a client first attempts to connect to an SSL server, it initiates the session by sending a **ClientHello** message to the server. The **ClientHello** message starts the SSL communication between the two systems. The **ClientHello** message contains some of the following components:

- Version: The version field contains the highest SSL version that the client supports.

- Random: A random number generated by the client.

- Session ID: An arbitrary sequence of bytes chosen by the server; it identifies a particular SSL session. The client may attempt to resume a previously established session by sending a non-zero session ID.

- Cipher suites: Identifies the list of ciphers suites that the client supports.

- Compression: Identifies the list of compression methods that the client supports.

ServerHello

If the server is able to find an acceptable set of algorithms, it responds to the **ClientHello** message with a **ServerHello** message. The server may use the **ServerHello** message to allow a resumed session. The **ServerHello** message contains some of the following components:

- Version: The version field contains the highest SSL version supported by both the client and server.

- Random: A random number generated by the server.

- Session ID: Identifies a particular SSL session. If the client sends a non-zero session ID and the server locates a match in its cache, the server will attempt to respond with the same value as was supplied by the client, and resume the session using the same cipher suite.

- Cipher suites: Identifies the cipher suite chosen by the server from the list of ciphers that the client supports.

- Compression: Identifies the compression method chosen by the server from the list that the client supports.

Certificate

The server sends its **Certificate** message containing the server's certificate or list of (chain) certificates, depending on the selected cipher suite.

Note: The server may send a **ServerKeyExchange** message when the server **Certificate** message does not contain enough data to allow the client to exchange a premaster secret. This is true of some ciphers such as **DHE-DSS**.

ServerHelloDone

After sending its certificate, the server sends a **ServerHelloDone** message, indicating it is done with handshake negotiation.

ClientKeyExchange

The client sends the **ClientKeyExchange** message containing the **PreMasterSecret**. The **PreMasterSecret** is sent encrypted using the public key of the server.

ChangeCipherSpec

Both the client and server send the **ChangeCipherSpec** message after the security parameters have been determined. The **ChangeCipherSpec** message activates the negotiated SSL options for the session. From this point forward, all messages are authenticated and encrypted. This stage is significant as it indicates that subsequent records will be protected under the newly negotiated CipherSpec and keys.

Finished

Each party sends a **Finished** message under the new algorithm, keys and secrets. The **Finished** message indicates that the handshake is complete, and the parties may begin to exchange application layer data.

TLS Record Protocol

The TRANSPORT LAYER SECURITY (TLS) Record protocol secures application data using the keys created during the Handshake. The Record Protocol is responsible for securing application data and verifying its INTEGRITY and origin. It manages the following:

- Dividing outgoing messages into manageable blocks, and reassembling incoming messages.

- Compressing outgoing blocks and decompressing incoming blocks (optional).

- Applying a MESSAGE AUTHENTICATION CODE (MAC) to outgoing messages, and verifying incoming messages using the MAC.

- Encrypting outgoing messages and decrypting incoming messages.

At the lowest layer of TLS protocol architecture and it relies on reliable transport protocol (TCP). It provide connection security parameters (symmetric encryption, DES 3DES RC4, MD5 or SHA) per session. TLS Record protocol is used to encapsulate various higher level protocols such as TLS Handshake protocols.

Record Protocol operation

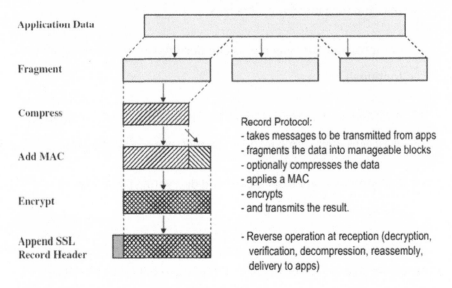

Application Data

Fragment

Compress

Add MAC

Encrypt

Append SSL
Record Header

Record Protocol:
- takes messages to be transmitted from apps
- fragments the data into manageable blocks
- optionally compresses the data
- applies a MAC
- encrypts
- and transmits the result.

- Reverse operation at reception (decryption,
  verification, decompression, reassembly,
  delivery to apps)

Figure 1-6

The Record Protocol takes messages to be transmitted, fragments the data into manageable blocks (2 upper right 14=16384 bytes, upper limit for the length of Record protocol's Payload Data), optionally compresses the data (encrypted size <= 1024 bytes), applies a MAC, encrypts, and transmits the result. Received data is decrypted, verified, decompressed, and reassembled, then delivered to higher level clients.

If a TLS implementation receives a record type it does not understand, it should just ignore it.

.

Basic Cryptography

So far we have managed to explain how to setup SSL and make a secure connection without understanding any of the core cryptographic engines working away under the hood. For the vast majority of readers that should be just fine and you can skip this next section if you don't wish to be bored to death on cryptography methods, algorithms and techniques. For some though, security technicians, consultants and engineers knowing about these crypto modules is not an option as you need to know about them at least at the high level as we will discuss in this next section.

Encryption algorithms or ciphers are mathematical formulas or functions applied to data to transform the plaintext or cleartext information, into an unintelligible format commonly referred to as ciphertext. An encryption algorithm generally has two inputs: a *key* and the plaintext itself.

The goal of a good encryption algorithm is to make the time it would take to decipher the ciphertext without the key, so long that it would greatly exceed the time-value of the original plaintext. Ideally, a strong algorithm and key combination should take at least millions of years to break, based on mathematical predictions. Of course the actual security is totally reliant on the keys staying secret.

Much of security is predicated on strong methods of keeping encryption keys sacrosanct as without the keys attackers are forced to rely upon brute-force methods, such as trying every possible key combination. However as we will see that shouldn't be underestimated as even seemingly huge key combinations can be tried out surprisingly quickly as we will see on fast computers. Therefore an ideal algorithm is strong, meaning that the algorithm itself is relatively impervious to direct attack, leaving attempts to derive or guess the key as the only practical avenue to breaking the encryption. Furthermore, the ideal encryption algorithm creates unique ciphertext from the same plaintext for each key permutation.

So when we talk about encryption what exactly is a key? In encryption a key is simply a number with a predetermined length. Keys can be created or generated in many ways, but computers commonly generate them as they can produce pseudo random numbers. Ideally, each key is truly random, meaning that any possible key combination is equally likely and that keys are not generated in a predictable fashion. The key length or modulus determines how many combinations are possible, and is commonly expressed in bits. The number of key combinations is 2 raised to the power of the key modulus. For example, a 40-bit key has 2^{40}, or over a trillion, combinations. While this sounds like an extraordinary number, it is an insecure key size, as all possible combinations can be tried within mere minutes by modern computers.

Encryption Families

Encryption algorithms are divided into two family groups based upon whether they are symmetric or asymmetric. In symmetric key encryption both the sender and receiver use the same secret key to encrypt and decrypt the information. On the other hand in asymmetric key encryption, the sender and receiver each have distinct but mathematically related keys.

Symmetric Encryption

Symmetric encryption algorithms are primarily used for bulk encryption of data, such as an entire file, document, or bundle of transaction data. The two fundamental symmetric encryption techniques are *substitution* and *transposition*. Substitution and transposition ciphers are simple and very fast and they operate by *replacing* or transposing each character with another character, or moving it to another location in the text. However both methods on their own are pretty much useless today as cryptanalysis techniques can break their algorithms very easily. Instead modern day symmetric encryption algorithms use a combination of the two techniques called diffusion where characters in the cleartext are simultaneously substituted and transposed. Hence, diffusion algorithms obfuscate the original cleartext by not only substituting differing values for the plaintext characters, but also by spreading the characters throughout the ciphertext. A significant strength of many diffusion-based algorithms is that the same character will actually be encrypted into a different symbol based on its location in the plaintext and the data that precedes it.

Symmetric algorithms also can be categorized into *block* and *stream* ciphers. Block algorithms encrypt and decrypt a fixed-size block of cleartext and ciphertext, respectively, usually a multiple of 64 bits or 8 Bytes.

Stream ciphers, on the other hand, continuously encrypt any amount of data as it is presented, usually by mathematically combining the data with a *keystream,* which is an infinitely long key sequence that is generated based on a finite key starting value.

Another strong feature with symmetric algorithms is that they possess a property known as the Avalanche effect, in which even a one-bit change in the plaintext results in changes in approximately one-half of all the ciphertext bits. Symmetric ciphers are fast and very efficient in terms of their computer code size and memory overhead, which is becoming more important as encryption capabilities are extended to devices designed for the Internet of Things which have constraints on power, processor, and memory.

Data Encryption Standard (DES)

DES is a standardized and published encryption algorithm, approved by the U.S. Government in 1977 after considerable analysis. The genesis of DES is traced back to a cipher termed Lucifer, invented by Horst Feistel of IBM. It uses a 56-bit key, which is sometimes stored with additional parity bits, extending its length to 64 bits. DES is a block cipher and encrypts and decrypts 64-bit data blocks. Although at the time of its inception, the effort to crack a 56-bit key was considered so enormous as to prevent brute-force attacks, it is now considered insecure, and all government agencies must use algorithms with longer keys, as discussed below. Despite the obsolescence of DES due to its key length, it is quite elegant and the most cryptanalyzed algorithm in the world, withstanding all attacks on the algorithm itself.

RC4

RC4 is a stream cipher, also created in 1987, and its only complexity is in the generation of the keystream, which is potentially an infinitely long sequence of key values, which start with a 40- or 128-bit key, and a 24-bit initialization vector (IV). The actual encryption step is very simple; the keystream is combined with the plaintext in an XOR[8] operation. Using the same key and IV, the keystream is totally reproducible, so in practice the sender and receiver using this algorithm will each be generating an identical keystream. RC4 is ten times faster than DES.

RC5

RC5 is a fast, parameterized block cipher, with a variable block size (32, 64 and 128 bits), variable key size (0 to 2040 bits), and a variable number of rounds (0 to 255), or individual encryption steps. RC5 is patented by RSA. It can be used as a drop-in replacement for DES, with the block size set to 64 bits and the key size set to 56 bits.

Triple DES (3DES)

Triple DES is simply three successive encryptions with DES. It is possible to use either two or three distinct keys with 3DES. Thus, for the three-key case, one obtains the benefit of a 168-bit key space with the known strength of the DES algorithm. Performed correctly, 3DES is as unbreakable a secret-key algorithm as any known, but it is slow. 3DES is defined as ANSI standard X9.52, and has been widely used in commerce and government applications.

Advanced Encryption Standard (AES)

The National Institute of Standards and Technology (NIST) selected an algorithm called "Rjindael" on October 2, 2000 as the AES in a multi-year competition. AES replaced DES. AES is projected to provide secure encryption of sensitive but unclassified government information until 2020. Rjindael is a fast block cipher, with variable key length and block sizes (each can be independently set to 128, 192 or 256 bits). AES became an official U.S. Government standard in 2002. Like DES before it, AES is now widely used for commercial and private encryption purposes. One significant benefit of AES is that the algorithm is public, and its use is unrestricted, with no royalties or license fees owed to the inventors or the government.

In summary symmetric keys are very fast and simple hence their suitability for encryption of large bodies of text, music and video. However, symmetric algorithms have an Achilles heel in that no matter how hard people have tried they just have not been able to get around the huge problem of how to distribute the shared secret key – securely.

Public Key Encryption

As we have seen symmetric algorithms have a significant drawback and that is how to securely distribute the shared key to intended receivers. However, in 1976, Hellman hit upon a simple scheme that, for the first time in history, allowed two parties to independently derive the same secret key without needing to transfer confidential information. Finally, the key distribution problem had been solved, a watershed event in cryptography. This key distribution method, known as Diffie-Hellman (DH) Key Exchange, is still used today.

Diffie-Hellman Key Exchange

The way Diffie-Hellman works is that **the parties are not** SHARING INFORMATION **during the key exchange they are** CREATING A KEY **together over an unsecured communications link.** This is an important distinction as Diffie-Hellman is a way of GENERATING a shared secret between two people in such a way that the secret can't be seen by observing the communication.

Diffie-Hellman is particularly useful because you can use this technique to create an encryption key with someone, and then start encrypting your traffic with that key. And even if the traffic is recorded and later analyzed, there's absolutely no way to figure out what the key was, even though the exchanges that created it may have been visible. This is where the term perfect forward secrecy comes from. Nobody analyzing the traffic at a later date can break in because the key was never saved, never transmitted, and never made visible anywhere.

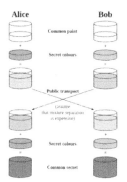

The way it works is reasonably simple as it uses the same underlying principles as public key cryptography, this is NOT asymmetric cryptography because nothing is ever encrypted or decrypted during the exchange. If you take a look at figure xxx you can get a good pictorial illustration of how this comes about. It is, however, an essential building-block, and was in fact the base upon which asymmetric crypto was later built.

Figure 1-7

The basic idea works like this:

1. I come up with two prime numbers g and p and tell you what they are.

2. You then pick a secret number (a), but you don't tell anyone. Instead you compute g^a *mod* p and send that result back to me. (We'll call that **A** since it came from **a**).

3. I do the same thing, but we'll call my secret number b and the computed number **B**. So I compute g^b *mod* p and send you the result (called "**B**")

4. Now, you take the number I sent you and do the exact same operation with *it*. So that's B^a *mod* p.

5. I do the same operation with the result you sent me, so: A^b *mod* p.

The "magic" here is that the answer I get at step 5 is *the same number* you got at step 4. Now it's not really magic, it's just math, and it comes down to a fancy property of modulo exponents. Specifically:

A good analogy is that if two people go out to buy beer, and one buys four six-packs, while the other buys six four-packs, they will return with the same number of beers: 24. The order of the multiplication operations does not affect the result: 6 x 4 beers = 4 x 6 beers = 24 beers

Or if you prefer a more formal explanation then:

$$(g^a \bmod p)^b \bmod p = g^{ab} \bmod p$$
$$(g^b \bmod p)^a \bmod p = g^{ba} \bmod p$$

Which, if you examine closer, means that you'll get the same answer no matter which order you do the exponentiation in? So I do it in one order, and you do it in the other. I never know what secret number you used to get to the result and you never know what number I used, but we still arrive at the same result.

That result, that number we both stumbled upon in step 4 and 5, is our shared secret key. We can use that as our password for AES or Blowfish, or any other algorithm that uses shared secrets. And we can be certain that nobody else, nobody but us, knows the key that we created together.

The Diffie-Hellman algorithm was so successful as a means of key exchange that it is also the foundation for a very modern method called Elliptical Curve Diffie-Hellman (ECDH), which is commonly supported today in servers and browsers. ECDH can be considered as an analogous scheme based on addition of points on an elliptic curve. In both schemes, the actual mechanisms are remarkably similar with the basic operations combined to create a primitive function known as a keyed one-way function. A keyed one-way function is a function that takes two inputs, one of which is private (e.g., the key), and produces one output. Given the two inputs, it must be straightforward to calculate the output but computationally infeasible to determine the key even if given the other input and the output.

This technique also relies on the basic rule of the 24 beers where the order of multiplication doesn't affect the end result so that 6 x 4 = 4 x 6 = 24 beers.

It is this property of integer-point multiplication that allows the parties to the ECDH exchange to agree upon a key, while it is the one-way property of the elliptic-curve primitive that allows them to accomplish this while keeping the keys and the result of the exchange secret from all but themselves.

The ECDH technique uses a very similar method to exchange keys as the original D-H in so much as the parties first agree on some base values for system parameters, a, b, p and G. This may be achieved by simply agreeing upon a standard set of parameters, such as those defined by the NIST P-256 standard, though it is highly advisable to calculate your own large prime numbers.

With the base keys agreed upon, each party then generates a random integer to use as its private key. For Alice, this is m, and for Bob it is n. Each then multiplies the base-point, G, by their private key to form a new point that represents their public key. This is the same method used as D-H except we have to remember that each point here comprises an x coordinate and a y coordinate on the elliptical curve. Then both parties exchange their public keys and subsequently multiply the other's public key by their own private key. Once again this is similar to the D-H method and this produces a new point on the elliptical curve, which is the same for each party. It remains only to convert this point to a bit string suitable for use as a key. As with the original D-H key exchange method an eavesdropper may be able to observe the agreed parameters and may even see the exchange of the public keys but they will not be able to determine what either private key is, nor the generated key that the two parties have agreed upon.

Static ECDH

As we described earlier, Diffie-Hellman style key-agreement schemes do not provide out-of-the-box authentication indeed often one of the desirable features may be to not authenticate the other party. However, in business this is a severe limitation but it can be overcome by each party disclosing their public keys in the form of a certificate from a public-key certification authority. If this type of operation is undertaken then we call this static ECDH, the static arises from the fact that the parties' key-pairs change only infrequently. Alas, there is perhaps a problem and that is because if both parties exchange their public keys as input then there will no longer be any random input to the scheme other than the parties' private keys. What does happen then is that the resulting agreed key is the same every time the same two parties communicate. Obviously, this is not very desirable from a security point of view as if there should be a compromise it is not just today's session that has been compromised but also all historical communications are also compromised. Hence, it is for this reason that it is a common choice not to use certificates, but to generate new key pairs for each run of the protocol and this technique is referred to as Anonymous ECDH.

Because anonymous ECDH does not provide entity authentication, there has to be another method that provides that vital function. Therefore, ECDH is often used in conjunction with a separate authentication scheme, such as a crypto-hash based system that uses digital signatures. This combination is called ephemeral ECDH, or ECDHE for short. Used in this way, ECDHE can provide Perfect Forward Secrecy.

Perfect Forward Secrecy

Perfect Forward Secrecy is a very topical and desirable feature especially in the realm of privacy and surveillance and what it actually means is that disclosure of the key used to protect one message cannot lead to the disclosure of keys protecting other messages, and that there is no single secret value whose compromise can lead to the compromise of multiple messages. Hence, there is no blanket access to all historical databases of messages, only the present message has been compromised and its contents disclosed. Therefore for securing encrypted messages that are at rest in a data repository etc PFS is a very desirable feature and it is present in ECDHE.

RSA Public Key Algorithm

The RSA algorithm was the work of Ronald Rivest, Ari Shamir and Leonard Adleman, all researchers at MIT and the inventors of the public key encryption algorithm.

In its simplest form RSA is a modern algorithm used by computers and browsers to encrypt and decrypt messages. It is an asymmetric cryptographic algorithm, which means that there are two different keys, one public key and one private key. Hence, RSA is also called public key cryptography, because the public key can be issued for public release. The other key, the private key must be kept secret.

RSA is a modern popular method of encryption with the added benefit of authentication as the public key can be used to decrypt the private key of the sender thereby authenticating that the message was encrypted by the sender's private key. Hence, if the sender signs a message using their private key this provides both authentications and non-repudiation as they later cannot claim not to have signed or sent the communication.

To explain in very simplistic terms how digital signing works let us suppose that Alice wants to send Bob an important confidential legal document. To this end Alice uses Bob's public key to send him an encrypted message. However, Bob has no way of verifying that the message was actually sent by Alice since anyone has access to Bob's public key, hence anyone could of sent him the encrypted message. This is a basic authentication problem so we need a method to authenticate Alice as the sender. So in order to verify the origin of a message, RSA can also be used to sign the message.

Subsequently, should Alice wish to send another encrypted message to Bob she can attach a "signature" by using a hash value and adding this to the message and signing with her private key. When Bob receives the signed message, he uses Alice's public key to decrypt the signature and then compares the resulting hash value with the message's actual hash value. If the two agree, he knows that the author of the message was in possession of Alice's secret key, and that the message has not been tampered with since it was signed with Alice's secret key.

As we have seen RSA is used for encryption, authentication and non-repudiation due to the flexibility of its public/private keys. The way RSA works at a very high level is that we need to find some prime numbers from which to generate our keys:

So in step 1, we can choose 2 prime numbers:

and we call these p & **q** so that **p** = 29, **q** = 31 (of course in the real world these would be extremely large prime numbers)

Then we need to start generating our public keys, which will be made up of n and e.

So let us calculate **n = p * q** = 29 * 31 = 899

and then calculate **t** = (**p** -1) * (**q** – 1) = (29 – 1) * (31 – 1) = 840

We then need to choose another prime number we will call **e**.

Our choice of e needs to be relatively prime to **t**. (i.e. **t** cannot be divisible by **e**) so let us pick 11

We now have n = 899 and e = 11 as the public key

We now need to make our secret key which will comprise n and d, we already have computed n therefore we need to find **d**.

To find d we will use this formula : **d * e** [=] 1 mod **t**

What this means is that we need to find a value for d that when (**d** * 11) / **t** will give us a remainder of one. So if we for example use the number 611 just by guesswork then (611 * 11) = 6721,

6721/840 = 8 with remainder 1. So 611 will work for d.

We now have everything we need for a private and public key to encrypt our data.

p – 29

q – 31

n – 899

t – 840

e – 11

d – 611

Our public keys becomes **n** and **e**

The private keys becomes **n** and **d**

We give our public key numbers (n and e) to the person that wants to send us their message. Their RSA algorithm will encrypt the message with the formula:

C = M^e mod n

C is our encrypted Message. So for example if the character to be encrypted was the letter 'w' whose ascii value is 119 then:

C = 119^{11} mod 899 = 595

The value of 595 is transmitted to the server.

In order to decrypt the message we need our private key (**n** and **d)**

Keep in mind we don't give anybody our private key.

We use the formula **M = C^d mod n**

so **M** = 595^{611} mod 899 = 119

M = 119 whose character value is 'w' which was the original message encrypted by a public key and decrypted using the secret key.

Note the fundamental differences between asymmetric and symmetric key encryption. When using secret key ciphers, there is a different secret key for each pair of parties communicating. In the public key case, there is just one key pair for each receiver, because the public key can be distributed to everyone who wants to send encrypted data to the receiver. Having the public key allows senders to encrypt data, but without the private key, they are unable to use the public key to decrypt communications from anyone else using the same key pair. Of course this is hugely advantageous from a scalability perspective as now you can support hundreds or millions of clients using one public/private key pair. But there is also a big downside in that should that private key be compromised then every single client's transactions are also compromised. Hence, we cannot stress enough the importance of keeping that secret key safe!

ECDSA – Elliptical Curve Digital Signature Algorithm

Since the introduction of SSL by Netscape in 1994, certificates for web sites have typically used a public/private key pair based on the RSA algorithm. As the SSL specification evolved into TLS, additional support for a wider variety of public key algorithms was added. One of the supported algorithms is ECDSA which is based on elliptic curves.

One of the major issues with SSL/TLS has always been the computational cost of the cryptography required on web servers to meet high demand. Consequently, service providers and enterprises that support huge numbers of servers are always on the lookout for a technology that can relieve them of the burden of handling SSL overhead. Hence, when a new technique based upon elliptic curves was touted as an efficient low demand alternative to RSA in SSL there was much interest.

A more recent alternative to the standard RSA encryption used in traditional SSL is Elliptic Curve Cryptography (ECC) and it is one of the more promising technologies in this area. Indeed the new boy on the block ECC-enabled TLS is faster uses far less CPU cycles and overhead, and is far more scalable on servers whilst provides the same or better security than the default cryptography in use on the web.

ECC 256-bit not only makes use of a more advanced encryption algorithm that is 64,000 times harder to crack than the standard RSA 2048-bit, but its use of a smaller key (only 256 bits long) means that it requires far fewer CPU cycles to encrypt the data. That can help you reduce costs and improve website performance. If desired, you can also combine the ubiquitous RSA root with the stronger security and server performance offered by ECC in our hybrid SSL/TLS certificates.

In SSL/TLS the certificate is digitally signed by a trusted certificate authority that validates the identity of the site owner. However, despite the number of options available since the transition to TLS, almost all certificates used on the web today are still RSA-based. This is because web sites have been slow to adopt new algorithms because they want to maintain support for legacy browsers that don't support the new algorithms. However since 2012 ECC signed certificates have seen a large upturn and now all the major certificate authorities are offering ECC signed certificates or hybrids which use an RSA root but are then signed with an ECC key.

For most web sites, security provided by 2,048-bit RSA keys is sufficient. The RSA public key algorithm is widely supported, which makes keys of this type a safe default choice. At 2,048 bits, such keys provide about 112 bits of security. If you want more security than this, note that RSA keys don't scale very well. To get 128 bits of security, you need 3,072-bit RSA keys, which are noticeably slower. ECDSA keys provide an alternative that offers better security and better performance. At 256 bits, ECDSA keys provide 128 bits of security. A small number of older clients don't support ECDSA, but modern clients do. It's possible to get the best of both worlds and deploy with RSA and ECDSA keys simultaneously if you don't mind the overhead of managing such a setup.

However ECC techniques are not without their issues as one interesting quirk of the ECDSA algorithm is that every signature requires some random or unpredictable data as input. If the source of randomness is predictable to an attacker, then they can figure out the private key. Hackers have exploited this vulnerability in several high-profile incidents.

The amount of randomness or entropy that a computer can generate is down to the number of unpredictable random actions that it encounters and this is typically through peripherals such as a mouse and keyboard which provides plenty of random seed data. Unfortunately with SSL private key generation and ECDSA which require deep entropy pools in order to generate sufficiently random numbers the servers that these keys are typically generated from have low entropy pools. For this reason some administrators prefer to create these keys on trusted machines with known high entropy though even on headless Linux servers with no peripherals there should always be sufficient entropy for ECDSA and SSL key generation in the /dev/urandom file.

However having said that in 2010, a flaw in the way random numbers were used in ECDSA on Sony's Playstation 3 resulted in a private key being leaked. More recently, some Android devices were found to be incorrectly generating random values, resulting in a massive theft of Bitcoins from devices running Bitcoin software.

Cryptographic Hashes

The basic concept of cryptographic hashes is that they are mathematical functions which take data as input and convert that input into a fixed length irreversible alphanumeric string called a message digest, hash value or digital fingerprint. The latter provides us a clue as to the value of cryptographic hashes as initially it is not clear why you would want to convert a message (plaintext) into an illegible alphanumeric fixed string if the process was irreversible. And that is cryptographic hashes main feature that the input cannot be determined from the output even if you know the hash that was used to create it. And that is the key difference between hashing and encryption. Cryptographic hashing must be a one-way process by definition whereas encryption is a two-way (reversible) process by necessity. After all there is no point sending someone an encoded message that they cannot decode.

The feature of irreversibility, even when the hash function is known, and the hashed output is to hand is a key feature in the security benefits we get from hash values. How this works is way beyond this book but a popular analogy relates to the fact that the process basically destroys any trace of the input, such as "Think of a random number, and then divide it by two. You will be left with 0 or 1 now try and work back to find the number you thought off." Of course this would be extremely difficult as every even or odd number divided by 2 is going to provide the output 0 or 1.

Another interesting feature and a difference with encryption is that cryptographic hashes always return a fixed length string regardless of the input size. For example, a whole book or just a short sentence being hashed through MD5 would produce an output of 128 bit regardless of the input size. Therefore unlike encryption where there is a direct relationship between the input size and length to the resulting encrypted output no such inference can be made from crypto-hashes fixed length output.

Additionally, the deterministic nature of cryptographic hashes results in the same input always returns the same alphanumeric string – exactly, and it must do this every time. Therefore, you must be able to hash the same paragraph of text and always receive exactly the same output string. Furthermore, no two non-identical inputs must ever return the same alphanumeric output. So every different and non-identical paragraph of text you feed into the hash function will return a different output string of a fixed length.

As a result a hash can be considered as a kind of signature or as is more commonly come across as a check-sum for file lengths in computing. For example, Linux file systems use the MD5 hash to compute a check-sum for downloads so that the files integrity can be verified, i.e. if even one bit has been tampered with in the source file the resultant check-sum will be significantly different and noticeable at a glance. And this is one of hashes strengths that we can use it to hash documents, download files, and letters to provide assurance that the originals have not been tampered with in any way during transit or storage.

Another purpose is in computer security when storing passwords in a database. If passwords are stored in clear text they are highly vulnerable to any security breach – yet many large companies still do this. Even if the passwords are encrypted there is still the additional CPU overheads, latency and the potential that they can be decrypted. With crypto-hashed passwords that option of reversing the hash-value string back to a readable password no longer exists so the hashed passwords are useless to anyone other than the system itself. Why that is comes about from a simple trick. When the user creates their password initially, the password they type is not stored but fed as the input string through a hash function, which converts the password to a hashed alphanumeric string which is duly stored in the database. On subsequent visits the user enters their password and it is once again passed through the same hash function to obtain a string output which can now be compared against the string stored in the database. If they match perfectly the user is authenticated if they do not match their access is denied.

Now there are two distinct types of hash functions that we are interested in, cryptographic hash functions and hash functions. In short all cryptographic hash functions are hash functions but not all hash functions are cryptographic hashes. The important differentiation is in their strength and this is measured on their ability to address some of the inherent concerns with cryptographic hashing.

Collision Resistance

The inherent value of a cryptographic class hash function is down to its reliability to accurately maintain the uniqueness between a fixed input and a hashed output. There should be extremely high confidence that only an identical input could produce the same hashed output. If there are occurrences of different inputs creating matching outputs then this is known as a collision and is extremely bad news. Hence we use collision resistance to judge the effectiveness and strength of a hash, as not all hash functions are of cryptographic strength. Indeed some start out intended for cryptography but are eventually discovered to have known instances of collisions, such as MD4 and MD5, which renders them unsuitable for cryptographic class use.

Collision resistance is determined by how difficult it is to create two different messages that will provide the same hashed output – regardless of the value. Obviously if it can be demonstrated that it is possible then confidence in the hashed function will be lowered and possibly no longer accepted in business or law.

The second issue that cryptographic hashes have to address is a technique called Preimage where an attacker will try to construct a message that will hash to a given value. Preimage is the opposite of collision in some ways as it is working backwards from an ideal, given hashed value to try and construct a matching message. The value of preimage to an attacker is that if they are able to "work backwards" from a hash and create some text that produces the **same** hash, they can use this to beat hashed passwords. They will not know the password but they will still gain entry to the system.

There is another version of Preimage where the attacker knows the actual input for example an application source file on the internet, and they wish to change the content of that file without altering the hashed value i.e. to prevent anyone noticing that they have tampered with the files code. This is called secondary reimaging and is considered to be theoretically easier to accomplish.

In order to evaluate the strengths and weaknesses of hash functions and their potential usefulness in cryptographic applications such as SSL, hash functions are tested for:

Preimage resistance

1. preimage resistance (given a hash h it must be difficult to find a message m that yields h when hashed)

2. weak collision resistance (given a message m1 it must be difficult to find a different message m2 so that m1 and m2 yield the same hash)

3. strong collision resistance (it should be difficult to find any messages m1 and m2 that yield the same hash)

The term difficult is not some wooly qualitative definition it does have a clearly defined mathematical meaning in this context such that it refers to 2^n for preimage and second preimage resistance, and $2^{(n/2)}$ for collision resistance. While we can't prove that the problem is indeed that hard, a cryptographic hash function is considered broken, once there are provable ways to better the brute-force techniques performance.

As a consequence of these rules cryptographic hash functions strengths are relative to their fixed lengths and so a hash function of 128 bit is considered to be weaker than one of 512 bit as there are trillions more potential combinations to work through when conducting a brute-force attack.

Of course 128 bits is still a huge combination of brute force attempts:

The possible hashes available: from a 128-bit hash can have 3.4×10^{38} possible values, which is:

340,282,366,920,938,463,463,374,607,431,768,211,456 possible hashes

Other hashes have even more bits: the SHA-1 algorithm generates 160 bits, whose output space is four billions times larger than that produced by MD5's 128 bits. Yet both of these crypto-hashes are no longer considered to be cryptographic strength hashes and should no longer be used within SSL cipher-suites.

Some of the more popular hashes we are likely to come across are:

- MD4 (128 bits, which is now obsolete in cryptography)

- MD5 (128 bits, which is also depreciated as a cryptographic hash function, but still seen in the wild)

- RIPEMD-160 (160 bits)

- SHA-1 (160 bits, is also listed to be depreciated, so it is highly recommended to stop supporting it within a cipher-suite, though it will be in the wild for years to come)

- SHA-256, SHA-384, and SHA-512 (longer versions of SHA-1, which are recommended with slightly different designs)

The Technical Differences between SSL/TLS

For most people SSL is the default term used to describe all three protocols and is used synonymously in conversation. Indeed many in the industry attest to the notion that they are the same, and that TLSv1.0 is in fact SSLv3.1 a continuation of SSLv3.0 but just under another working group. However in documentation we often see more precise references to each which can cause confusion, especially when you have Google asking do you want SSL or TLS.

The differences between the two protocols are very minor and technical, but they **are** different standards. TLS uses stronger encryption algorithms and has the ability to work on different ports. Additionally, which is important distinction is that TLS version 1.0 does not interoperate with SSL version 3.0 so the terms shouldn't be used synonymously hence the precision of language in technical documentation.

As some general background about how this confusion arose we need to take a quick glance back to the dawn of the internet. In the early 90's the SSL protocol was developed at Netscape to enable ecommerce transactions to be conducted security over the internet. There was a requirement for encryption to protect the customers' personal data, as well as authentication of the ecommerce sites servers and strong message integrity to guarantee a safe transaction. Netscape's answer to the vulnerabilities of internet transactions was the SSL protocol.

Netscape envisaged a secure transport layer sitting directly on top of TCP enabling protocols above it (HTTP, email, instant messaging, and many others) to operate unchanged while providing communication security when communicating across the network. Hence the specification's of SSL was developed to provide this secure socket layer.

Consequently, SSL can support many applications and when SSL is used correctly, an eavesdropper can only view the encrypted tunnel so they are limited to knowing the connection endpoints, type of encryption, as well as the frequency and an approximate amount of data sent, but cannot read or modify any of the actual data.

SSL 2.0 was the first publicly released version of the protocol, but it was replaced by SSL 3.0 due to a number of potential security vulnerabilities. Because the SSL protocol was proprietary to Netscape, the IETF formed an effort to standardize the protocol, resulting in RFC 2246, which was published in January 1999 but was not compatible with SSLv3. Subsequent security flaws in SSL3.0 highlighted in devastating fashion by the attack POODLE as good as consigned SSLv3.0 to the bucket.

Since then, the IETF has continued iterating on the TLS protocol to address security flaws, as well as to extend its capabilities: TLS 1.1 (RFC 2246) was published in April 2006, TLS 1.2 (RFC 5246) in August 2008, and work is now underway to define TLS 1.3.

As of 2015, all SSL versions are considered broken and insecure and TLS is now ubiquitous.

The differences between the TLS protocol and SSL are not dramatic, but they are significant enough that TLS 1.0 and SSL 3.0 do not interoperate. Some other technical differences are:

1. Protocol Version in Messages - To differentiate TLS Version 1.0 and SSL Version 3.0, the protocol version number negotiated by a client and server communicating through TLS Version 1, is version number (3.1)

2. Alert Protocol Message Types - The following message types are those that are allowed as Alert Descriptions within the TLS protocol. Upon examination of the list, one would notice that "NoCertificate" has been removed from the SSL list, since it is assumed that if no certificate exists for the user, there is no need for a separate message. TLS uses the assumption that the client can return an empty certificate message if it does not have a certificate to use. Additionally, several more descriptions have been added to bring the number of Alert Descriptions to 23 from 12.

3. Message Authentication TLS implements a standardized MAC (H-MAC) that has been proven in many other implementations. The main benefit to this change is that H-MAC operates with any hash function, not just MD5 or SHA, as explicitly stated by the SSL protocol.

4. Key Material Generation TLS uses the HMAC standard and its pseudorandom function (PRF) output to generate key material. Each system starts with a premaster secret; next, it creates the master secret. Then it generates the required key material. The

major difference is that SSL uses RSA, Diffie-Hellman or Fortezza/DMS output to create key material. This output generates secret information based on the CipherSuite and Parameters selected during session negotiations.

5. CertificateVerify In SSL, the CertificateVerify message requires a complex procedure of messages. With TLS, however, the verified information is completely contained in the handshake messages previously exchanged during the session.

6. Finished in TLS, the PRF output of the H-MAC algorithm is used with the master secret and either a "client finished" or a "server finished" designation to create the Finished message. In SSL, the finished message is created in the same ad-hoc manner that key material is generated: using a combination of hash output, selected ciphersuite and parameter information.

7. Baseline Cipher Suites As mentioned earlier, SSL specifically supports RSA, Diffie-Hellman and Fortezza/DMS ciphersuites. TLS has stopped allowing Fortezza/DLS support, but allows for ciphersuites to be added to the protocol in future revisions.

How SSL and TLS provide authentication

Now that we have a better understanding of the cipher techniques and algorithms used by SSL/TLS we can take a deeper dive into how it actually secures data transmissions for many types of protocols and not just web traffic. We can also understand what role each of the ciphers play in providing the security functions of secure key exchange, authentication, confidentiality and data integrity. Therefore in this section we will once again consider the important handshake process that constructs a SSL/TLS session and we will see how these security functions are achieved.

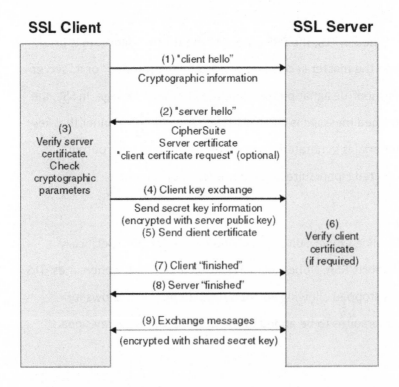

If we consider the diagram in figure 1-7

In overview, the steps involved in the SSL handshake are as follows:

1. The SSL or TLS client sends a "client hello" message that lists cryptographic information such as the SSL or TLS version and, in the client's order of preference, the CipherSuites supported by the client. The message also contains a random byte string that is used in subsequent computations. The protocol allows for the "client hello" to include the data compression methods supported by the client.

2. The SSL or TLS server responds with a "server hello" message that contains the CipherSuite chosen by the server from the list provided by the client, the session ID, and another random byte string. The server also sends its digital certificate. If the server requires a digital certificate for client authentication, the server sends a "client certificate request" that includes a list of the types of certificates supported and the Distinguished Names of acceptable Certification Authorities (CAs).

3. The SSL or TLS client verifies the server's digital certificate.

4. The SSL or TLS client sends the random byte string that enables both the client and the server to compute the secret key to be used for encrypting subsequent message data. The random byte string itself is encrypted with the server's public key.

5. If the SSL or TLS server sent a "client certificate request", the client sends a random byte string encrypted with the client's private key, together with the client's digital certificate, or a "no digital certificate alert". This alert is only a warning, but with some

implementations the handshake fails if client authentication is mandatory.

6. The SSL or TLS server verifies the client's certificate. The SSL or TLS client sends the server a "finished" message, which is encrypted with the secret key, indicating that the client part of the handshake is complete.

7. The SSL or TLS server sends the client a "finished" message, which is encrypted with the secret key, indicating that the server part of the handshake is complete.

8. For the duration of the SSL or TLS session, the server and client can now exchange messages that are symmetrically encrypted with the shared secret key

We can start to gain an appreciation of how SSL/TLS achieves server authentication. In step 1) the client uses the server's public key to encrypt the data that is used to compute the secret key. The server can generate the secret key which is used for subsequent symmetric encryption only if it can decrypt that data with the correct private key.

For client authentication, which is rarely used, the server uses the public key in the client certificate to decrypt the data the client sends during step 5 of the handshake. The exchange of finished messages that are encrypted with the secret key (steps 7 and 8 in the overview) confirms that authentication is complete.

If any of the authentication steps fail, the handshake fails and the session terminates.

The exchange of digital certificates during the SSL or TLS handshake is part of the authentication process. The parties exchange certificates as required as follows, where CA X issues the certificate to the SSL or TLS client, and CA Y issues the certificate to the SSL or TLS server:

For server authentication only, the SSL or TLS server needs:

- The personal certificate issued to the server by CA Y

- The server's private key

and the SSL or TLS client needs:

- The CA certificate for CA Y

If the SSL or TLS server requires client authentication, the server verifies the client's identity by verifying the client's digital certificate with the public key for the CA that issued the personal certificate to the client, in this case CA X. For both server and client authentication, the server needs:

- The personal certificate issued to the server by CA Y

- The server's private key

- The CA certificate for CA X

and the client needs:

- The personal certificate issued to the client by CA X

- The client's private key

- The CA certificate for CA Y

Both the SSL or TLS server and client might need other CA certificates to form a certificate chain to the root CA certificate.

What happens during certificate verification

As we saw in figure xxx during steps 3 and 6, the SSL/TLS client verifies the server's certificate, and the SSL /TLS server verifies the client's certificate. There are four aspects to this verification:

1. The digital signature is checked

2. The certificate chain is checked therefore there must be intermediate CA certificates present

3. The expiry and activation dates and the validity period are checked.

4. The revocation status of the certificate is checked

Secret key reset

During an SSL or TLS handshake a *secret key* is generated to encrypt data between the SSL or TLS client and server. The secret key is used as a symmetric encryption key for fast efficient data encryption, this is simply because public key encryption is great for initial creation of the secure tunnel but is too slow for encrypting the main communication flow therefore the secret key is used to provide symmetric encryption that is applied to the data to transform bulk plaintext into unreadable ciphertext, and ciphertext into plaintext.

The way the server/client creates the secret key is that it is generated from the random text sent as part of the handshake and that key will be used to encrypt the plaintext into ciphertext. The secret key is also used in the MAC (Message Authentication Code) algorithm, which is used to determine the data integrity and whether a message has been altered or tampered with in any way during transmission.

If the secret key is discovered, the plaintext of a message could be deciphered from the ciphertext, or the message digest could be calculated, allowing messages to be altered without detection. Even for a complex algorithm, the plaintext can eventually be discovered by applying every possible mathematical transformation to the ciphertext. To minimize the amount of data that can be deciphered or altered if the secret key is broken, the secret key can be renegotiated periodically. When the secret key has been renegotiated, the previous secret key can no longer be used to decrypt data encrypted with the new secret key.

How SSL and TLS provide confidentiality

SSL and TLS use a combination of symmetric and asymmetric encryption to ensure message privacy. During the SSL or TLS handshake, the SSL or TLS client and server agree an encryption algorithm and a shared secret key to be used for one session only. All messages transmitted between the SSL or TLS client and server are encrypted using that algorithm and key, ensuring that the message remains private even if it is intercepted. SSL supports a wide range of cryptographic algorithms. Because SSL and TLS use asymmetric encryption when transporting the shared secret key, there is no key distribution problem.

How SSL and TLS provide integrity

SSL and TLS provide data integrity by calculating a message digest using a cryptographic hash function such as SHA-2. Using an SSL/TLS secure connection does ensure data integrity, provided that the CipherSpec in your channel definition uses an appropriate hash algorithm such as SHA-2 or above. In particular, if data integrity is a concern, you should avoid choosing a CipherSpec whose hash algorithm is listed as "None". Use of MD5 is also strongly discouraged as this is now very old and no longer secure for most practical purposes. (MD5 is considered depreciated and should not be used, SHA1 is also considered no longer suitable for cryptographic purpose and should be dropped in favour of SHA-2 or higher)

Working with Cipher-Suites

Now that we have a working knowledge of many of the ciphers that we use in modern SSL/TLS transmissions we can start on the thorny issue of which ones to enable and use as a matter of preference. This might sound at first a bit strange as surely you would simple enable the strongest ciphers for each function: authentication, encryption and data integrity and disable the others on the web server or browser. Unfortunately, with the internet being as it is a global community that is merely wishful thinking. Indeed even if you only intended to have your web-server communicate within national borders you will still find a vast number of seemingly obsolete browsers and indeed web-servers that still require or support older ciphers.

Therefore in their wish to accommodate all potential visitors to their sites, especially ecommerce sites, server administrators are loathed to intentionally restrict visitors' access. After all this is potentially lost trade and no one wants that. The solution therefore is not to disable older ciphers but to still offer them for use with older browsers by including them within a cipher-suite.

A cipher-suite is simply a menu of supported combinations of ciphers for key exchange, encryption and integrity that are listed in order of preference with the strongest/preferred combo of ciphers offered first and the weakest supported combo offered as a last resort.

Now this is all very well but as we know some ciphers are no longer considered cryptographic class anymore, for example MD5 and RCA4 which only a few years ago were the bedrock of SSL/TLS and still supported by many browsers – both old and new. And here is the thing, it is not just the server administrator that has the problem of which ciphers to support it is also a headache for the browser vendors. This is because there are still vast amounts of servers out in the wild running on old versions of SSL and using depreciated ciphers and despite huge publicity surrounding security flaws and vulnerabilities i.e. BEAST, Heartbleed and POODLE seemingly refuse to or are incapable of upgrading their systems. As a result, browser vendors must still support older ciphers or their customers would not be able to connect to older servers or to servers perhaps in less advanced nations. Of course this is not something vendors want to happen as it is their product that will get the blame. Consequently, we arrive at the cipher-suite solution of offering and supporting a wide range of combinations whilst still trying to maintain the strictest levels of security.

Cipher-Suites in action

To see how the cipher-suite works in your browser when it negotiates a secure connection in the wild you can simply go to
https://cc.dcsec.uni-hannover.de/
And you will receive back a list of the supported and preferred ciphers that you current browser supports. For example this is the list for Firefox 52.1.1

Cipher Suites Supported by Your Browser (ordered by preference):

Spec	Cipher Suite Name	Key Size	Description
(c0,2b)	ECDHE-ECDSA-AES128-GCM-SHA256	128 Bit	Key exchange: ECDH, encryption: AES, MAC: SHA256.
(c0,2f)	ECDHE-RSA-AES128-GCM-SHA256	128 Bit	Key exchange: ECDH, encryption: AES, MAC: SHA256.
(cc,a9)	ECDHE-ECDSA-CHACHA20-POLY1305-SHA256	256 Bit	Key exchange: ECDH, encryption: ChaCha20 Poly1305, MAC: SHA256.
(cc,a8)	ECDHE-RSA-CHACHA20-POLY1305-SHA256	256 Bit	Key exchange: ECDH, encryption: ChaCha20 Poly1305, MAC: SHA256.
(c0,2c)	ECDHE-ECDSA-AES256-GCM-SHA384	256 Bit	Key exchange: ECDH, encryption: AES, MAC: SHA384.
(c0,30)	ECDHE-RSA-AES256-GCM-SHA384	256 Bit	Key exchange: ECDH, encryption: AES, MAC: SHA384.
(c0,0a)	ECDHE-ECDSA-AES256-SHA	256 Bit	Key exchange: ECDH, encryption: AES, MAC: SHA1.
(c0,09)	ECDHE-ECDSA-AES128-SHA	128 Bit	Key exchange: ECDH, encryption: AES, MAC: SHA1.
(c0,13)	ECDHE-RSA-AES128-SHA	128 Bit	Key exchange: ECDH, encryption: AES, MAC: SHA1.
(c0,14)	ECDHE-RSA-AES256-SHA	256 Bit	Key exchange: ECDH, encryption: AES, MAC: SHA1.
(00,33)	DHE-RSA-AES128-SHA	128 Bit	Key exchange: DH, encryption: AES, MAC: SHA1.
(00,39)	DHE-RSA-AES256-SHA	256 Bit	Key exchange: DH, encryption: AES, MAC: SHA1.
(00,2f)	RSA-AES128-SHA	128 Bit	Key exchange: RSA, encryption: AES, MAC: SHA1.
(00,35)	RSA-AES256-SHA	256 Bit	Key exchange: RSA, encryption: AES, MAC: SHA1.
(00,0a)	RSA-3DES-EDE-SHA	168 Bit	Key exchange: RSA, encryption: 3DES, MAC: SHA1.

Further information:

User-Agent:	Mozilla/5.0 (Windows NT 5.1; rv:52.0) Gecko/20100101 Firefox/52.0
Preferred SSL/TLS version:	TLSv1.2
SNI information:	cc.dcsec.uni-hannover.de
SSL stack current time:	The TLS stack of your browser did not send a time value.

This connection uses TLSv1.2 with ECDHE-RSA-AES128-GCM-SHA256 and a 128 Bit key for encryption.

As can be seen from Figure 1-8 The Firefox browser is currently supporting a list of cipher-suite options with each one making up a combination of protocol, key exchange, encryption and what are called MAC protocols. The first few are self explanatory, in that they handle the choice of protocol (Pr), secure key exchange (Kx) and encryption (En), and key size (bits) respectively. The latter term MAC is not as intuitive as it refers to the hashing algorithm used for TLS/SSL data packets integrity and authentication checks the most common of which is SHA1 (which is due to be depreciated).

The list in Figure 1-8 is ordered by preference with respect of the Firefox browser and the actual connection is not the first preferred suite offered by Firefox but instead it has negotiated the connection parameters to be: 'This connection uses TLSv1.2 with ECDHE-RSA-AES128-GCM-SHA256 and a 128 Bit key for encryption.'

Different browser vendors support other cipher-suites so for comparison on the same machine but using Google Chrome Version 49 this is the list of preferred cipher-suites and the actual negotiated connection parameters:

Cipher Suites Supported by Your Browser (ordered by preference):

Spec	Cipher Suite Name	Key Size	Description
(cc,a8)	ECDHE-RSA-CHACHA20-POLY1305-SHA256	256 Bit	Key exchange: ECDH, encryption: ChaCha20 Poly1305, MAC: SHA256.
(cc,13)	ECDHE-RSA-CHACHA20-POLY1305-SHA256	256 Bit	Key exchange: ECDH, encryption: ChaCha20 Poly1305, MAC: SHA256.
(c0,2f)	ECDHE-RSA-AES128-GCM-SHA256	128 Bit	Key exchange: ECDH, encryption: AES, MAC: SHA256.
(c0,14)	ECDHE-RSA-AES256-SHA	256 Bit	Key exchange: ECDH, encryption: AES, MAC: SHA1.
(c0,13)	ECDHE-RSA-AES128-SHA	128 Bit	Key exchange: ECDH, encryption: AES, MAC: SHA1.
(00,9c)	RSA-AES128-GCM-SHA256	128 Bit	Key exchange: RSA, encryption: AES, MAC: SHA256.
(00,35)	RSA-AES256-SHA	256 Bit	Key exchange: RSA, encryption: AES, MAC: SHA1.
(00,2f)	RSA-AES128-SHA	128 Bit	Key exchange: RSA, encryption: AES, MAC: SHA1.
(00,0a)	RSA-3DES-EDE-SHA	168 Bit	Key exchange: RSA, encryption: 3DES, MAC: SHA1.

Further information:

User-Agent:	Mozilla/5.0 (Windows NT 5.1) AppleWebKit/537.36 (KHTML, like Gecko) Chrome/49.0.2623.112 Safari/537.36
Preferred SSL/TLS version:	TLSv1.2
SNI information:	cc.dcsec.uni-hannover.de
SSL stack current time:	The TLS stack of your browser did not send a time value.

This connection uses TLSv1.2 with ECDHE-RSA-AES128-GCM-SHA256 and a 128 Bit key for encryption.

Figure 1-9

As we can see the selection of cipher-suites is very similar, the exception being that Chrome doesn't support ECDSA hence the order of preference varies a lot from Firefox. The result is that the preferred connection is established using:

'TLSv1.2 with ECDHE-RSA-AES128-GCM-SHA256 and a 128 Bit key for encryption'

The choices of ciphers that are included in the cipher-suites for each category are:

Key exchange and Authentication algorithms:

RSA

Rivest, Shamir, Adleman

DH

Diffie-Hellman

DHE

    Diffie-Hellman Ephemeral

ECDH

    Elliptic-Curve Diffie-Hellman

KRB5

    Kerberos

SRP

    Secure Remote Password Protocol

PSK

    Pre-shared key

DSA

    Digital Signature Algorithm

ECDSA

    Elliptic Curve Digital Signature Algorithm

DSS

    Digital Signature Standard

Encryption and MAC algorithms:

3DES

    Triple Data Encryption Algorithm

AES

    Advanced Encryption Standard

Camelia

    Block cipher developed by Mitsubishi and NTT

DES

    Data Encryption Standard

Fortezza

> Security token based cipher

GOST

> Block cipher developed in USSR

IDEA

> International Data Encryption Algorithm

RC2

> Rivest Cipher 4

RC4

> Rivest Cipher 2

SEED

> Block cipher developed by Korean Information Security Agency

SHA

> Secure Hash Algorithm

MD5

> Message Digest algorithm 5

When you are referencing cipher suites it is quite common to see examples such as in figure 2-0

0x000017	TLS_DH_Anon_EXPORT_WITH_RC4_40_MD5	TLS	DH	Anon	RC4_40	40	MD5
0x000018	TLS_DH_Anon_WITH_RC4_128_MD5	TLS	DH	Anon	RC4_128	128	MD5
0x000019	TLS_DH_Anon_EXPORT_WITH_DES40_CBC_SHA	TLS	DH	Anon	DES40_CBC	40	SHA
0x00001A	TLS_DH_Anon_WITH_DES_CBC_SHA	TLS	DH	Anon	DES_CBC	56	SHA

Figure 2-0

The important point to note here are the terms EXPORT and Anon. The term EXPORT means that it is a deliberately hamstrung cipher of very limited key size certified for use outside of the US at a time in the 90's when export of cipher technology was heavily restricted. If we look at each of the items in figure xxx, for example SSL id 0x17 and 0x19 both are described as EXPORT and so have key lengths of only 40 bits – export restrictions limited ciphers to below 56 bits. As we can see in the non-Export versions SSL id 0x18, 0x1A that although they still have anonymous authentication they have key lengths of 128 and 56 bits respectively. The take away here is to avoid these ciphers as they are deliberately weakened and almost certainly have state agency access.

A complete exhaustive list of all the published RFC cipher-suite combinations can be found here:

http://www.thesprawl.org/research/tls-and-ssl-cipher-suites/

Server-side Cipher-suites

In order to communicate securely, you must first ascertain that you are communicating directly with the desired party (and not through someone else who will eavesdrop on the communications) and that you are exchanging data securely. In SSL and TLS, cipher suites define how secure communication takes place. They are composed from various building blocks with the idea of achieving security through diversity. If one of the building blocks is found to be weak or insecure, you should be able to switch to another.

You should rely chiefly on the Encryption with Associated Data (AEAD) suites that provide strong authentication and key exchange, forward secrecy, and encryption of at least 128 bits. Some other, weaker suites may still be supported, provided they are negotiated only with older clients that don't support anything better.

There are several obsolete cryptographic primitives that MUST be avoided:

- Anonymous Diffie-Hellman (ADH) suites do not provide authentication.

- NULL cipher suites provide no encryption.

- Export cipher suites are insecure when negotiated in a connection, but they can also be used against a server that prefers stronger suites (the FREAK attack).

- Suites with weak ciphers (typically of 40 and 56 bits) use encryption that can easily be broken.

- RC4 is insecure.

- 3DES is slow and weak.

Use the following suite configuration, designed for both RSA and ECDSA keys, as your starting point:

TLS_ECDHE_ECDSA_WITH_AES_128_GCM_SHA256

TLS_ECDHE_ECDSA_WITH_AES_256_GCM_SHA384

TLS_ECDHE_ECDSA_WITH_AES_128_CBC_SHA

TLS_ECDHE_ECDSA_WITH_AES_256_CBC_SHA

TLS_ECDHE_ECDSA_WITH_AES_128_CBC_SHA256

TLS_ECDHE_ECDSA_WITH_AES_256_CBC_SHA384

TLS_ECDHE_RSA_WITH_AES_128_GCM_SHA256

TLS_ECDHE_RSA_WITH_AES_256_GCM_SHA384

TLS_ECDHE_RSA_WITH_AES_128_CBC_SHA

TLS_ECDHE_RSA_WITH_AES_256_CBC_SHA

TLS_ECDH_ECDSA_WITH_AES_128_CBC_SHA256

TLS_ECDH_ECDSA_WITH_AES_256_CBC_SHA384

TLS_ECDH_ECDSA_WITH_AES_128_GCM_SHA256

TLS_ECDH_ECDSA_WITH_AES_256_GCM_SHA384

TLS_DHE_RSA_WITH_AES_128_GCM_SHA256

TLS_DHE_RSA_WITH_AES_256_GCM_SHA384

TLS_DHE_RSA_WITH_AES_128_CBC_SHA

TLS_DHE_RSA_WITH_AES_256_CBC_SHA

TLS_DHE_RSA_WITH_AES_128_CBC_SHA256

TLS_DHE_RSA_WITH_AES_256_CBC_SHA256

Warning

It is recommended that you always first test your TLS configuration in a staging environment, transferring the changes to the production environment only when certain that everything works as expected. Please note that the above is a generic list and that not all systems (especially the older ones) support all the suites. That's why it's important to test first.

The above example configuration uses standard TLS suite names. Some platforms use nonstandard names; please refer to the documentation for your platform for more details. For example, the following cipher-suite names would be used with OpenSSL:

ECDHE-ECDSA-AES128-GCM-SHA256

ECDHE-ECDSA-AES256-GCM-SHA384

ECDHE-ECDSA-AES128-SHA

ECDHE-ECDSA-AES256-SHA

ECDHE-ECDSA-AES128-SHA256

ECDHE-ECDSA-AES256-SHA384

ECDHE-RSA-AES128-GCM-SHA256

ECDHE-RSA-AES256-GCM-SHA384

ECDHE-RSA-AES128-SHA

ECDHE-RSA-AES256-SHA

ECDHE-RSA-AES128-SHA256

ECDHE-RSA-AES256-SHA384

DHE-RSA-AES128-GCM-SHA256

DHE-RSA-AES256-GCM-SHA384

DHE-RSA-AES128-SHA

DHE-RSA-AES256-SHA

DHE-RSA-AES128-SHA256

DHE-RSA-AES256-SHA256

Each protocol (TLSv1.0, TLSv1.1, TLSv1.2, etc) provides its own set of cipher suites. The preferred protocol today should be the latest version of TLS namely TLSv1.2. With this version of TLS there is inbuilt support for over 300 cipher-suites. However, supporting all those is unnecessary and potentially hazardous as there are still many weak combinations supported, i.e. MD5 and RC4. After all the strength of the encryption used within a TLS session is determined by the encryption cipher negotiated between the server and the browser. Therefore, to ensure that only strong cryptographic ciphers are negotiated and then selected it is essential that the server must be modified to disable the use of weak ciphers and then to present the remaining strong ciphers in a logical order of preference. It is also recommended to configure the server to only support strong ciphers and to use sufficiently large key sizes. In general, the following general rules for servers should be observed when selecting cipher suites:

1. Use the very latest recommendations, as they may be volatile these days
2. Setup your policy to get a white-list for recommended ciphers,
3. Activate to set the cipher order by the server, e.g. 'SSLHonorCipherOrder On'
4. Highest priority for ciphers that support 'Forward Secrecy' (-> Support ephemeral Diffie-Hellman key exchange)
5. Favor GCM over CBC regardless of the cipher size. In other words, use Authentication
6. Use encryption algorithms with Associated Data (AEAD), e.g. AES-GCM, AES-CCM.
7. Watch also for stream ciphers which XOR the key stream with plaintext
8. Priorize the ciphers by the sizes of the cipher and the MAC

9. Use SHA2 or above for digests,

10. Disable weak ciphers without disabling legacy browsers and bots that have to be supported (find the best compromise),

11. If you are forced to support legacy operating systems, libraries or special business applications you may need to add 3DES (=TLS_RSA_WITH_3DES_EDE_CBC_SHA, =DES-CBC3-SHA, 0x0A) with very low priority for a transition time. Be ready to phase it out (status as of Feb 2017). It is **not** recommended to use 3DES together with perfect forward secrecy ciphers (DHE, ECDHE). Disable 3DES completely, if possible.

12. Disable cipher suites that do not offer encryption (eNULL, NULL)

13. Disable cipher suites that do not offer authentication (aNULL). aNULL includes anonymous cipher suites ADH (Anonymous Diffie-Hellman) and AECDH (Anonymous Elliptic Curve Diffie Hellman).

14. Disable export level ciphers (EXP, eg. ciphers containing DES)

15. Disable key sizes smaller than 128 bits for encrypting payload traffic

16. Disable the use of MD5 as a hashing mechanism for payload traffic

17. Disable RC4 cipher suites

18. DHE-ciphers should be usable for DH-Pamameters >= 2048 bits, without blocking legacy browsers (The ciphers 'DHE-RSA-AES128-SHA' and 'DHE-RSA-AES256-SHA' moved to the end as some browsers like to use them but are not capable to cope with DH-Params > 1024 bits; alternative option suppress these ciphers).

19. ECDHE-ciphers must not support weak curves, e.g. less than 256 bits.

20. Define a cipher string that works with different versions of your encryption tool, like openssl

SSL Self-Signed Certificates

Up until now, we have been discussing SSL and CA signed trusted certificates, which any major web browser will recognize due to the effect of certificate chain. These trusted certificates are a necessity for secure and trusted communication over the internet and are not optional, they are a necessity for websites involved in ecommerce, email or for financial transactions. This point cannot be stressed enough SSL CA Certificates should be used for any communications over insecure media when personal or sensitive information is being transmitted. Many websites do not do this even when user credentials are being exchanged. Furthermore, SSL provides user confidence that the site they are communicating with is who or what they claim to be.

This is all very good for communicating over the web, but that if you just want to secure communications between two applications over the LAN or WAN, or where encryption is the primary driver and authentication a secondary concern. SSL CA certificates would be a very expensive solution perhaps justifiable depending on the value of the transactions but now that we have grounding in ciphers and protocols a better way is to sign our own certificates for internal system communications. To clarify though, self-signed certificates should never be used for public web servers and used with caution even with private intranet web applications. However self-signed certificates do have their uses in server to server communications such as in encrypting and securing a MySQL server for instance. To understand how self signing a certificate works we need to examine how SSL certificates work.

How do you know that you are dealing with the right person or rather the right web site? Well, someone has taken great length (if they are serious) to ensure that the web site owners are who they claim to be. This someone, you have to implicitly trust: you have his/her certificate loaded in your browser (a root Certificate). A X.509 digital certificate, which contains information about the owner of the certificate, like their e-mail address, the owner's name, certificate usage, duration of validity, resource location or Distinguished Name (DN), which includes the Common Name (CN) (web site address or e-mail address depending of the usage) and the certificate ID of the person who certifies (signs) this information. It contains also the public key and finally a hash to ensure that the certificate has not been tampered with. As you made the choice to trust the person who signs this certificate, therefore you also trust this certificate. This is a certificate trust tree or certificate path. Usually your browser or application has already loaded the root certificate of well known Certification Authorities (CA) or root CA Certificates. The CA maintains a list of all signed certificates as well as a list of revoked certificates. A certificate is insecure until it is signed, as only a signed certificate cannot be modified. However, you can sign a certificate using itself; it is called a self-signed certificate. All root CA certificates are self-signed.

Making a Self-Signed Certificate

You will probably never want to use a self-signed SSL certificate on a public web server but they do have their uses. For instance, self-signed certificates are fine for:

- **Self-signed certificates can be used on a development server**. There is no need to spend extra cash buying a trusted certificate when you are just developing or testing an application.

- **Self-signed certificates can be used on an intranet**. When clients only have to go through a local intranet to get to the server, there is virtually no chance of a man-in-the-middle attack.

- **Self-signed certificates can be used on personal sites with few visitors**. If you have a small personal site that transfers non-critical information, there is very little incentive for someone to attack the connection.

Once you have OpenSSL installed, just run this one command to create an Apache self signed certificate:

```
openssl req -x509 -nodes -days 365 -newkey rsa:2048 -keyout
mysitename.key -out mysitename.crt
```

You will be prompted to enter your organizational information and a common name. The common name should be the fully qualified domain name for the site you are securing (www.mydomain.com). You can leave the email address, challenge password, and optional company name blank. When the command is finished running, it will create two files: a mysitename.key file and a mysitename.crt self signed certificate file valid for 365 days.

Install Your Self Signed Certificate

Now, you just need to configure your Apache virtual host to use the SSL certificate. If you only have one Apache virtual host to secure and you have an ssl.conf file being loaded, you can just edit that file. Otherwise, you will need to make a copy of the existing non-secure virtual host, paste it below, and change the port from port 80 to 443.

1. Open your Apache configuration file in a text editor. Depending on your operating system and Apache version, it will be located in different places but you will usually find it at /etc/httpd/httpd.conf. On a Windows machine, you will usually find it at C:\Program Files\Apache\Apache2\conf\httpd.conf

2. In most cases, you will find the <VirtualHost> blocks in a separate file in a directory like /etc/httpd/vhosts.d/ or /etc/httpd/sites/. Add the lines in bold below.

3. <VirtualHost 192.168.0.1:**443**>
    DocumentRoot /var/www/website
    ServerName www.yourdomain.com
    SSLEngine on
    SSLCertificateFile /etc/ssl/crt/mysitename.crt
    SSLCertificateKeyFile /etc/ssl/crt/mysitename.key
    </VirtualHost>

4. Change the names of the files and paths to match your certificate files. Save the changes and exit the text editor.

5. Restart your Apache web server using one of the following commands: /usr/local/apache/bin/apachectl startssl /usr/local/apache/bin/apachectl restart

To create a self-signed certificate in ISS simply use the GUI and follow the steps below:

1. In **Features** view, double-click **Server Certificates**.
2. In the **Actions** pane, click **Create Self-Signed Certificate**.
3. On the **Create Self-Signed Certificate** page, type a friendly name for the certificate in the **Specify a friendly name for the certificate** box, and then click **OK**.

On the other hand, you can create your self-signed certificate online using this self-signed cert generator, by going here:

http://www.selfsignedcertificate.com/

SSL Certificate Management

Organizations use SSL certificates and encryption keys to protect communications across the Internet, enabling web technologies such as secure online banking, bill payment and e-commerce the internet services we've come to expect. Of course, ecommerce isn't the only use for SSL certificates: Organizations rely heavily upon SSL certificates to encrypt data and authenticate systems and applications—both inside and outside the corporate network.

Encryption implementations work reliably when properly configured and deployed, therefore many organizations don't realize until it is often too late that they are not managing their encryption implementations as well as they should. This is because, SSL certificates and encryption keys aren't the easiest things in the world to manage—especially using manual processes—and this contributes to their widespread neglect. Unfortunately, there are few business processes, which are as important, yet neglected, as effective enterprise key and certificate (EKCM) management.

Problems that arise because of poor SSL certificate management reside in categories that correspond to the EKCM lifecycle, namely: discovery, enrollment, monitoring, validation, notification, provisioning, remediation, reporting and revocation.

Discovery

You can't manage certificates if you don't know about them, so you must create a comprehensive certificate and key inventory. The discovery process feeds this inventory by telling you:

- Discover what certificates you have: Most large organizations are unaware of the number of certificates they have deployed. Most often, this discrepancy is due to various internal teams issuing certificates from multiple internal and external certificate authorities (CA).

- Discover which certificate authority (CA) issued each certificate: This information is critical to recovering from CA compromises— of which there have been several in the past few years. You must also know how many self-signed certificates you have in your encryption deployment.

- Discover when each certificate is set to expire: Expired certificates are bad news, as they cannot be extended after they expire, so a new certificate will have to be issued. This either causes unplanned system outages or opens a door into the network, or both.

- Discover what the key strength for each certificate in use is: Weak key algorithms leave your organization vulnerable to those who can masquerade their actions as valid activity on the network.

To discover and record the most useful information and store it in an SSL certificate inventory, the discovery process should includes finding encryption algorithms and key lengths for each certificate. Obviously, manually collecting this sort of detailed information is tedious, time-consuming and error-prone (If you undertake manual discovery, be sure to check with managers who may have deployed certificates for department-specific applications without going through your IT organization.)

Enrollment

Enrollment is the process of submitting a certificate-signing request (CSR) to either an external or internal CA. Your enrollment process should:

- Guide requestors by specifying the domain name, certificate configurations and CAs they can use.

- Restrict the number of administrators who are authorized to request certificates, implementing dual controls (separation of duties) where possible to prevent rogue certificates from infiltrating your network.

You should begin the enrollment process well before the date existing certificates expire or you plan to bring new services online. To do this, you'll need to monitor existing certificates' expiration dates.

Provisioning

The provisioning process is closely related to enrollment. It includes steps such as:

- Creating keystores to house certificates and private keys (and keystore backups)

- Configuring keystore parameters

- Distributing intermediate root certificates (intermediate root—or CA certificates—validate certificate chains; it's very important to install the right intermediate root certificates in the right certificate keystores)

- Generating certificates' key pairs

- Obtaining CA approvals (often a CA requirement)

- Retrieving and installing issued certificates

- Distributing certificates and keys (for many-to-one implementations, such as load-balancing)

Validation

Validation involves making sure certificates are correctly installed, configured and working properly. This process also entails checking to make certain certificates comply with your organization's policies. Again, you'll need to know the status of every certificate anyone in your organization has deployed—a level of knowledge that you can acquire only by investing a great deal of time and effort if you manually manage certificates.

Monitoring

After you've created a comprehensive inventory of the SSL certificates and keys on your network, you must use your inventory system to monitor important events, such as impending expiration dates.

Notification

The person who (or process that) monitors your certificates must notify responsible parties in time to replace soon-to-expire certificates, or certificates that have inadequate key lengths, weak algorithms or were issued by a compromised CA (a condition that requires immediate notification).

Remediation

When responsible parties receive notifications, they must remedy the issues that engendered them. For example, depending upon the type of notification a responsible party receives, he or she may need to:

- Revoke certificates (from rogue or compromised CAs, for example)

- Enroll new certificates (when current certificates will soon expire, for example)

- Notify stakeholders (when a breach occurs, for example)

- Perform other steps to remedy SSL-related problems (replace weak key length certificates, for example)

Reporting

Internal security policies and external regulations demand accountability. When your organization deals with protected or regulated information (such as personal health information), you must be able to demonstrate compliance.

This entails creating reports to document events, such as authorized or unauthorized access to your keystores. You can obtain data for reports manually, by scouring event logs and other resources—including your comprehensive inventory—or you can automate the reporting process.

Revocation

Closely related to the remediation process, revocation is the final stage in the EKCM lifecycle. You should always revoke certificates that compromised CAs have signed, for example. In addition, you should revoke expiring certificates that you're replacing so they don't become targets for hackers.

Manually performing the aforementioned processes takes an estimated 4.5 hours per year per certificate. If your organization has only a thousand certificates (and most have far more), you need at least two full-time employees to manually manage them. Because manual EKCM is so time and labor intensive (and, consequently, costly), and because manual processes are fraught with the potential for human error, your organization should seriously consider an automated solution.

SSL Vulnerabilities

SSL/TLS has been incredibly at the forefront of web communications now for over 20 years. This is an astonishing achievement for a protocol that was devices back in the mid-90s, at the very dawn of the internet. However, in that time SSL has grown and modules such as OpenSSL have burgeoned with options and switches which has made it flexible and hugely configurable. One important aspect that we must understand about SSL/TLS is that it is a highly effective security technique when deployed diligently but you should not have any false sense of security – SSL/TLS is as buggy as any other software, possibly more so due to its vast array of options, so there are plenty of vulnerabilities.

In February, 2017, the OpenSSL Project released an updated security advisory detailing 4 current and distinct vulnerabilities. The vulnerabilities are now addressed and are referenced here simply to highlight that SSL/TLS is no security panacea it need careful implementation and nurturing, it is not plug and play and certainly isn't fire and forget.

CVE-2017-3733 (OpenSSL advisory) [High severity] 16th February 2017:

During a renegotiation handshake if the Encrypt-Then-Mac extension is negotiated where it was not in the original handshake (or vice-versa) then this can cause OpenSSL to crash (dependent on ciphersuite). Both clients and servers are affected. Reported by Joe Orton (Red Hat).

- Fixed in OpenSSL 1.1.0e (Affected 1.1.0d, 1.1.0c, 1.1.0b, 1.1.0a, 1.1.0)

CVE-2017-3731 (OpenSSL advisory) [Moderate severity] 26th January 2017:

If an SSL/TLS server or client is running on a 32-bit host, and a specific cipher is being used, then a truncated packet can cause that server or client to perform an out-of-bounds read, usually resulting in a crash. For OpenSSL 1.1.0, the crash can be triggered when using CHACHA20/POLY1305; users should upgrade to 1.1.0d. For Openssl 1.0.2, the crash can be triggered when using RC4-MD5; users who have not disabled that algorithm should update to 1.0.2k Reported by Robert Święcki of Google.

- Fixed in OpenSSL 1.1.0d (Affected 1.1.0c, 1.1.0b, 1.1.0a, 1.1.0)

- Fixed in OpenSSL 1.0.2k (Affected 1.0.2j, 1.0.2i, 1.0.2h, 1.0.2g, 1.0.2f, 1.0.2e, 1.0.2d, 1.0.2c, 1.0.2b, 1.0.2a, 1.0.2)

CVE-2017-3730 (OpenSSL advisory) [Moderate severity] 26th January 2017:

If a malicious server supplies bad parameters for a DHE or ECDHE key exchange then this can result in the client attempting to dereference a NULL pointer leading to a client crash. This could be exploited in a Denial of Service attack. Reported by Guido Vranken.

- Fixed in OpenSSL 1.1.0d (Affected 1.1.0c, 1.1.0b, 1.1.0a, 1.1.0)

CVE-2017-3732 (OpenSSL advisory) [Moderate severity] 26th January

2017:

There is a carry propagating bug in the x86_64 Montgomery squaring procedure. No EC algorithms are affected. Analysis suggests that attacks against RSA and DSA as a result of this defect would be very difficult to perform and are not believed likely. Attacks against DH are considered just feasible (although very difficult) because most of the work necessary to deduce information about a private key may be performed offline. The amount of resources required for such an attack would be very significant and likely only accessible to a limited number of attackers. An attacker would additionally need online access to an unpatched system using the target private key in a scenario with persistent DH parameters and a private key that is shared between multiple clients. For example this can occur by default in OpenSSL DHE based SSL/TLS ciphersuites. Note: This issue is very similar to CVE-2015-3193 but must be treated as a separate problem. Reported by OSS-Fuzz project.

- Fixed in OpenSSL 1.1.0d (Affected 1.1.0c, 1.1.0b, 1.1.0a, 1.1.0)

- Fixed in OpenSSL 1.0.2k (Affected 1.0.2j, 1.0.2i, 1.0.2h, 1.0.2g, 1.0.2f, 1.0.2e, 1.0.2d, 1.0.2c, 1.0.2b, 1.0.2a, 1.0.2)

These are some of the current 2017 vulnerabilities against SSL/TLS but historically there have been several high profile cases despite the strong reputation of OpenSSL and other module suppliers. We will discuss several of the landmark vulnerabilities and attacks as they provide a good in depth look at the internal mechanics of SSL and how some of the underpinning security modules actually work in practice.

BEAST

"THE SSL PROTOCOL, AS USED IN CERTAIN CONFIGURATIONS IN MICROSOFT WINDOWS AND MICROSOFT INTERNET EXPLORER, MOZILLA FIREFOX, GOOGLE CHROME, OPERA, AND OTHER PRODUCTS, ENCRYPTS DATA BY USING CBC MODE WITH CHAINED INITIALIZATION VECTORS, WHICH ALLOWS MAN-IN-THE-MIDDLE ATTACKERS TO OBTAIN PLAINTEXT HTTP HEADERS VIA A BLOCKWISE CHOSEN-BOUNDARY ATTACK (BCBA) ON AN HTTPS SESSION, IN CONJUNCTION WITH JAVASCRIPT CODE THAT USES (1) THE HTML5 WEBSOCKET API, (2) THE JAVA URLCONNECTION API, OR (3) THE SILVERLIGHT WEBCLIENT API, AKA A "BEAST" ATTACK."

SSL had been considered a very secure protocol for decades and few actually seemed to question its reputation for robustness but of course SSL is only going to be as strong as the underpinning cybersuite that is deployed. This inherent weakness came to prominence when two researchers Thai Duong and Julian Rizzo demonstrated a proof of concept with their BEAST (*Browser Exploit Against SSL/TLS*) attack. However we should note that their exploit isn't necessarily an attack on SSL/TLS itself, but an attack on the way it's implemented in modern browsers (and servers). The BEAST attack itself only works against browsers and HTTPS. This doesn't mean, of course, that other record-splitting attacks don't exist, but this one does require a browser to work.

The BEAST attack is of interest as it is an attack on one of the core security blocks that underpin SSL/TLS and security encryption in general which is a well known weakness in how block ciphers work. Block ciphers as the name suggests work with blocks of data of specific size. For example the best known block cipher algorithm for many years was DES (Data Encryption Standard), which is not considered secure by today's standards as its block size is a mere 8 bytes, but even AES (Advanced Encryption Standard), which has longer block size and is today's security standard share the same inherent weakness – the fixed block size.

Block ciphers work by encrypting a specified block of data using a similar sized encryption key, which remains secret. Typically, an attacker eavesdropping on the transmission or conversation will only be able to view encrypted data which is of no use to them. However, there is a basic weakness in all block ciphers and that is a block of plain-text that is subsequently encrypted using a password must always return the same encrypted values i.e. regardless of the number of times we encrypt "the quick brown fox ..." it must always return the same encrypted values, for instance, "Ah06e4087e452187 ...". Now of course if you know some of the words in the phrase it doesn't help you at all. But if you knew for instance in the case of DES, a one 8 byte word that would be encrypted and transmitted as exactly one 8 byte block, then you have the potential to identify the encrypted value. So for example if the attacker could trick the victim into sending a known plain-text word that fell exactly on the 8 byte boundary, let's say, 'alasdair' then the attacker eavesdropping on the wire would have the encrypted code for that word 'A0 82 7B 63 45 23 3E 5D', which they could recognize any time it was used – if encrypted by the same password – in any future correspondence. Furthermore they could effectively decrypt that word – cyberblock- despite not knowing the encryption key.

Of course this weakness in block ciphers has been known for decades and the way to mitigate the issue was to use a technique called cipher block chaining (CBC). What this technique amounted to was that the original 8 byte block would be obfuscated by doing an XOR with a similar sized block of random data before the result was encrypted using the password. Now of course even if the attacker did manage to trick the victim into sending an 8 byte block of known data it would only be of use to them that one time as next time it would be XOR'ed with a different random block of data.

Of course this leaves the problem of where do you get the random block of data from. And the solution was pretty simple; before encrypting a block, combine it with the one that came before it in a way that can be easily reversed at decryption time. In the case of CBC, this combining is done by XOR-ing the block with the one that came before it — this makes separating it easy because XOR is self-reversing (that is: a xor b xor b = a). The problem with this of course is that if the attacker can capture packets by eavesdropping on the data flow and it is a trivial matter to rebuild the flow using any network analyser such as Wireshark as each TCP/IP packet has a sequence number. As a result the attacker could then theoretically use the last 8 bytes from the preceding packets to identify the data that was used in the XOR. It would still be of little or no use to them as they would only recognize the encrypted values of the words they already knew.

Because TLS was designed to be resistant against attackers who have compromised the communication channels in exactly this way such that they can modify or insert arbitrary traffic as they please, this type of attack was expected. Consequently, the TLS working group drafted a fix in 2006 with the introduction of TLS 1.1. The proposal was that each packet instead of using the preceding block for an XOR would get its own Initial Vector (IV), and that IV is transmitted (unencrypted) at the beginning of each packet. The fact that it's transmitted unencrypted is not a security problem as by the time the attacker can see it, it's already been used.

So how on earth did BEAST work if the TLS working group had put mitigating measures in place back in 2006? Well it transpires that despite the TLS's concern those in the industry where less enthused by such theoretical attacks and were slow to implement TLS 1.1 if they did at all. The result as history will show is that in 2011 Thai Duong and Julian Rizzo turned the theoretical in to a viable practical attack when they demonstrated their BEAST (*Browser Exploit Against SSL/TLS*) attack.

The way that Duong and Rizzo managed to get BEAST to work relied upon the weaknesses in cipher blocks, not just DES, but all cipher blocks. What they determined was that from the attackers perspective there are two major problems one is that they have to know or be able to guess an entire 8 block value in order to get anything out of the attack. And the only way to do that is to trick the victim into sending easily identifiable plain-text or rather what they presume or hope is the correct plain-text they are looking for.

The clever part was that Duong and Rizzo realized the solution was not tricking the victim to enter some known data as that really wasn't necessary using a browser attack because most HTTP requests are highly predictable. Indeed with a typical HTTP request such as this:

GET /index.html **HTTP/1.1**

Host: *mysite.com*

Cookie: Session=123456

Accept-Encoding: text/html

Accept-Charset: utf-8

Most if not all of the information is predictable, only the real prize of the session key is the unpredictable problem. However session IDs are longer and more diverse than this one (typically including alphanumeric values as well as punctuation characters) in the real world, but the combinatorial difference turns this into a mountable attack, as Rizzo and Duong demonstrated with real code.

Now, the problem should have been that the browser rejected their efforts. However, since HTTP mandates that each request to a cookie'd host include the cookie, then tricking the browser into sending the cookie in an easily determined location, is easy. What was tricky was getting the browser to inject known plaintext within a TLS record boundary after the CBC residue of the previous block was known. Rizzo and Duong exploited a security hole in the Java Applet of their browser to make this work.

What is important to take from this is that the BEAST is a vulnerability on the client side (web browser) and for this attack to be carried out successfully there are many requirements that need to fall into place. We should not mistake the threat as being theoretical but it does fall into the category of improbable as if an attacker had all the access and importantly the knowledge and skills they required to pull this attack off successfully they would almost always have had a myriad of easier and more potent potential attacks on offer.

Today BEAST is not considered to be a huge problem as all the major browser vendors have implemented fixes and OpenSSL versions 0.9.6d or later have implement a feature, in which an **empty TLS record** is sent immediately, before sending a message. This empty TLS record causes a change in the CBC state, as it triggers a **new IV** message, which the attacker cannot predict.

SSL/TLS implementers were slow and browser vendors not any better when it came to mandating the use of TLS 1.1 so around 70% of servers were vulnerable to the attack. However, to date (May 2017) there has never been a recorded BEAST attack in the wild. One quick solution that was touted at the time was to change from block cipher encryption to streaming ciphers and many did by swapping over to RC4, but that too was to have unforeseen issues.

CRIME

"In a CRIME attack, the attacker recovers the content of secret authentication cookies and uses this information to hijack an authenticated web session. The attacker uses a combination of plaintext injection and TLS compression data leakage to exploit the vulnerability. The attacker lures the Web browser to make several connections to the website. The attacker than compares the size of the ciphertexts sent by the browser during each exchange to determine parts of the encrypted communication and hijack the session."

CRIME (Compression Ratio Info-leak Made Easy) was created by security researchers Juliano Rizzo and Thai Duong, who cooked up the BEAST SSL exploit the previous year. The so-called CRIME technique lures a vulnerable web browser into leaking an authentication cookie created when a user starts a secure session with a website. Once the cookie has been obtained, it can be used by hackers to login to the victim's account on the site.

The cookie is deduced by tricking the browser into sending compressed encrypted requests to a HTTPS website and exploiting information inadvertently leaked in the process. Each sent request contains the cookie and some extra data that is tweaked by malicious JavaScript code. The change in size of the sent compressed messages is measured to determine the cookie's contents character by character.

Web users that have browsers that implement either TLS or SPDY compression are potentially at risk - but the vulnerability only comes into play if the victim visits a website that accepts the affected protocols. Support is widespread but far from ubiquitous.

The researchers worked with Mozilla and Google to ensure that both Firefox and Chrome are protected. Microsoft's Internet Explorer is not vulnerable to the attack, and only beta versions of Opera support SPDY. Smartphone browsers and other applications that rely on TLS may be vulnerable.

"Basically, the attacker is running a script on Evil.com," Rizzo explained to Kaspersky Labs' Threatpost. "He forces the browser to open requests to Bank.com by, for example, adding <img alt=""> tags with the src pointing to Bank.com. Each of those requests contains data from mixed sources."

Each encrypted request includes an image file name - a constantly changing detail that is generated by the malicious script; the browser's identification headers, which don't change; and the login cookie, and the target of the attack. When the file name matches part of the login cookie, the size of the message drops because the compression algorithm removes this redundancy.

"The problem is that compression combines all those sources together," Rizzo added. "The attacker can sniff the packets and get the size of the requests that are sent. By changing the [file name] path, he could attempt to minimise the request size, i.e.: when the file name matches the cookie."

This brute-force attack has been demonstrated against several sites including Dropbox, Github and Stripe. Affected organisations were notified by the pair, and the websites have reportedly suspended support for the leaky encryption compression protocols.

RC4 Vulnerabilities revealed

RC4 (Rivest Cipher 4) is a stream cipher algorithm which was by its nature immune to the threat of any BEAST attack and despite its own - by that time - dubious security credentials was hyped as the best solution to the cyber chain threat. Unfortunately RC4 was also a disaster waiting to happen even though RC4 has been around since the early nineties when it was a closely guarded trade-secret of RSA Security it was suspected of harboring its own vulnerabilities. During that time, the 90s, RC4 was widely deployed in browsers and web servers as it was fast and simple, but along with its popularity and industry acclaim it was quietly accumulating several disturbing security weaknesses of its own. Surprisingly, during all this time RC4 came under little scrutiny and it was generally considered to be secure even though it was known that it had some theoretical but impractical weaknesses. For example there had been many issues published regards its bias towards initial bit sequences making them predictable. Indeed although most of the vulnerabilities, which had been highlighted over the years were considered purely theoretical requiring samples of 2^{26} sessions or 13×2^{30} encryptions some later vulnerabilities and poor implementations such as in the disastrous WEP wireless security protocol had raised serious concerns.

Latterly, however RC4 has been found to be anything but secure, and many of the theoretical weaknesses are now considered to be practically realizable. An attack on RC4 in TLS and SSL that requires 13×2^{20} encryptions to break RC4 was unveiled on 8 July 2013 and later described as "feasible" in the accompanying presentation at a USENIX Security Symposium in August 2013.

In addition, revelations during 2013 by Edward Snowdon regarding state agency NSA security breaches also indicated a rather cozy relationship between RSA and the NSA leading many to believe that perhaps RC4 had perhaps allowed backdoors for state players.

Furthermore, in July 2015, subsequent improvements in the attack make it increasingly practical to defeat the security of RC4-encrypted TLS and as a result RC4 has been dropped from use by the TLS working group in 2015.

SSL and TLS are robust and ubiquitous protocols that provide the foundation for secure internet transaction. However, some implementations of SSL, such as OpenSSL have had their fair share of vulnerabilities over the past few years, the most notable of which was Heartbleed, a potentially devastating vulnerability.

What is the Heartbleed bug?

Heartbleed is simply a coding error in the OpenSSL package versions 1.0.1 which has been in the wild since March 2012 and in all versions up to and including 1.0.1f. The vulnerability allows an attacker to target SSL on port 443 and manipulate SSL heartbeats in order to read the memory of a system running a vulnerable version of OpenSSL. A Heartbeat is simply a keep-a-alive sent to ensure that the other party is still active and listening. Its use is to maintain the session parameters, the context, between the hosts. If SSL did not use heartbeats then the hosts would continually have to renegotiate security parameters, which is not efficient. So heartbeats are a good thing hence there widespread use in SSL.

The problem however was not with heartbeats themselves but with one line of code, which allowed an attacker to change the heartbeat size and fire it off using TCP on port 443. Unfortunately, as the code did not check the memory size boundaries, the attacker was able read up to 64KB of memory. By repeatedly changing the heartbeat size, and repeating the ploy, the attacker could obtain more 64KB blocks of data. The fix restricts the heartbeat payload boundary to 16KB and validates the entire heartbeat.

AS of OpenSSL package 1.0.1g released 7th April 2014 there is a latest fix to the OpenSSL module. Earlier versions are not affected. Therefore, only systems built during that period are likely to be affected by Heartbleed, unless, ironically, as a system administrator you have been adhering to best practices and following the latest upgrade path.

Mitigating the problem and upgrading the code then is easy, but that isn't really the major concern. It is what an attacker may have found in those 64K blocks of memory, which is the real problem. Was the attacker able to view passwords, credit card details, or other confidential information? Therefore, owners of compromised systems were advising their customers to change their passwords, though more as a precaution, that in the unlikely event, that their credentials had been stolen. However in order to get the message out to all their customers required socializing the vulnerability. Within hours, the mainstream media had picked it up and the newly named Heartbleed bug was front-page news.

It soon became apparent though that it was not really an unlikely event that customers' credentials may have been compromised, it was all too likely. Indeed, there were several demonstrations of passwords being captured doing the rounds on Twitter and other social media networks. This revelation, though disputed by some, clearly pointed towards another potential problem. This time it was a problem with catastrophic potential. Could the attacker get hold of the encryption keys?

As with all asymmetric encryption, it is vital that the SSL private keys remain secure. If the private key is compromised, or even suspected to have been, then so has the security. This of course had further ramifications, if the keys were compromised then so were the digital certificates, they would need to be revoked and new certificates generated by the trusted certificate authorities (CA), and that would be very costly. Many of the CAs' around the globe were rubbing their hands with glee in expectation of a major payday.

On their website, Heartbeat.com issued their advice to web-site owners

'These are the crown jewels, the encryption keys themselves. Leaked secret keys allow the attacker to decrypt any past and future traffic to the protected services and to impersonate the service at will. Any protection given by the encryption and the signatures in the X.509 certificates can be bypassed. Recovery from this leak requires patching the vulnerability, revocation of the compromised keys and reissuing and redistributing new keys. Even doing all this will still leave any traffic intercepted by the attacker in the past still vulnerable to decryption. All this has to be done by the owners of the services.'

The Heartbleed bug has potentially grave consequences for the security and ecommerce industries. Even just the potential of compromised encryption keys and certificates can erode trust and shake public confidence, and all this came about because of one small error in a single line of code.

What is Freak – and how is it resolved?

Researchers have identified a new SSL/TLS vulnerability, dubbed FREAK, which can be exploited to force an HTTPS connection to use weaker and easier to crack encryption – thus, potentially opening the doors for attackers to obtain private information such as usernames and passwords. "A connection is vulnerable if the server accepts RSA_EXPORT cipher suites and the client either offers an RSA_EXPORT suite or is using a version of OpenSSL that is vulnerable to CVE-2015-0204,"

Essentially, the FREAK vulnerability makes supposedly secure communications much less secure. The communications are crackable once the shorter key is discovered through brute force decryption. Furthermore, the exploit enables a range of secondary attacks on both clients and servers.

According to a Google statement, *"We encourage all websites to disable support for export certificates. Android's connections to most websites – which include Google sites, and others without export certificates – are not subject to this vulnerability. We have also developed a patch to protect Android's connection to sites that do expose export certs and that patch has been provided to partners."*

Safari and most Android-native browsers are vulnerable, but Chrome is not. These web clients are all built on open source, but make use of different versions of OpenSSL and employ different web application tool kits.

The origins of this vulnerability go back to the 1990s when the U.S. Government tried to place restrictions on the export of what it considered "weapons-grade" encryption. The theory went that U.S. domestic communication could benefit from 128-bit (and longer) keys, but foreign communications needed to be accessible to U.S. intelligence and law enforcement, and so should not have the strong encryption, therefore it could not be exported legally and weaker "export-grade" encryption was born.

Typically, a browser's client would determine that a web client and host would negotiate the strongest encryption "available," before falling back to a weaker "export" protocol only if required, which left a convenient back door for monitoring.

FREAK exploits this legacy behavior still present in between a quarter and third of all deployed web servers – a sad, but topical example of how implementing forced backdoors into encryption can certainly come back to haunt you.

Poodle attack kills SSL 3.0

Another entity that came back to haunt was the Cipher Block Chain attacks of which BEAST had been the poster child back in 2011, which had caused so much concern regards cyber block algorithms. Indeed in 2015, Google researchers announced that they had discovered another vulnerability that was very similar but simpler to practically exploit than BEAST and they called it POODLE. This new POODLE vulnerability was also targeting fixed cyber block mode algorithms, with JavaScript injections from websites into vulnerable browsers and attacking cookies. However, more worrying was that by this time 2015 JavaScript drive past attacks were now common place which made this POODLE attack far more practical that BEAST every was due to it not requiring any special Java browser plug-in.

The weakness of POODLE, however was that it was only effective on SSLv3, which by 2015 should have been a trivial matter as SSLv3 had been depreciated a decade previously. Unfortunately things don't work like this in the real world and many servers supporting SSL/TLS still did support SSLv3 as a fall back option. This is of course one of the big problems with offering lesser versions during negotiation because the net result can be falling back to insecure depreciated versions that are vulnerable. However, because some servers are configured poorly and don't implement version negotiation correctly, browsers break this mechanism by retrying connections with lesser SSL/TLS versions when TLS handshaking fails. What this meant in practice was that an attacker could by injecting some trivial errors on the network cause a browser to speak SSLv3 to any server and then negotiate an SSLv3 connection in order to run the above attack.

Once again the solutions were for the browser vendors to remove or disable by default support for SSLv3. On the server side there is also a requirement to remove support for SSLv3 so that they do not get involved in negotiations with SSLv3 speaking browsers. POODLE wouldn't be as serious without the ability of the active network attacker to downgrade modern browsers down to SSL 3. There's a solution to this problem, via the TLS_FALLBACK_SCSV indicator that must be supported by clients and servers in order to be effective. All the major browser vendors are now supporting this as is OpenSSL hence this should greatly reduce POODLES attack footprint considerably.

Lucky 13

As we have just witnessed SSL/TLS in CBC-mode has been the subject of several attacks over the years, most notably Poodle and the BEAST attacks. However, there are countermeasures for both of these attacks, and TLS in CBC-mode was once more believed to be secure once these countermeasures were applied. Unfortunately it appears that the advice to implementers in the TLS RFCs concerning how to avoid padding oracle attacks does not close all possible avenues of attack.

This became clear with the announcement of another proof of concept vulnerability that had been demonstrated by researchers at the Royal Holloway, University of London. What made this attack vector different was that the researchers created attacks on TLS 1.1 or 1.2, or with DTLS 1.0 or 1.2. The attacks also apply to implementations of SSL 3.0 and TLS 1.0 that incorporate countermeasures to previous padding oracle attacks and All TLS and DTLS ciphersuites which include CBC-mode encryption are also potentially vulnerable to attack.

Furthermore, this new attack, Lucky 13, uses timing of error messages to determine whether a decryption failure was detected. As the current notion of whether TLS Record Protocol meets a strong notion of cryptographic security, which assumes that an attacker cannot discern the cause of TLS decryption failures this attack casts doubt on the veracity of the notion.

Because of the many environmental issues that this attack must overcome, due mainly to network conditions such as delay and jitter, as there is a lot of noise on a LAN. It currently takes a great deal of samples to statistically determine the different error responses. For example, the way Lucky 13 operates is that the attacks rely on the fact, for certain carefully chosen message lengths and when the HMAC-SHA1 MAC algorithm is used, that TLS messages containing at least two bytes of correct padding will be processed slightly faster than TLS messages containing one byte of correct padding or padding that is incorrectly formatted. It is therefore possible to determine messages containing at least two bytes of correct padding from all other patterns by the induced network delay.

However, the lucky 13 attack is perhaps well named as although they are confident that they can perform a Man-in-the-Middle attacker to recover plaintext from a TLS/DTLS connection when CBC-mode encryption is used it would seem in the wild to be very optimistic. This is because, in the attack's simplest form, it can reliably recover a complete block of TLS-encrypted plaintext using about 2^{23} TLS sessions. Now, that is a huge amount of connections, and each TLS session needs reconnected as the session is broken when the error, the attack, is detected, which is every time as that is what they are measuring. Furthermore, it is assuming the attacker is located on the same LAN as the machine being attacked and HMAC-SHA1 is used as TLS's MAC algorithm.

SSL techniques in Application Development

SSL/TLS goes a long way to securing data communication between a client and a server however often failings in the application itself can contribute to vulnerabilities through insecure configurations. Some examples of the sort of problems we see all too frequently in web application especially in mobile apps are:

- Due to insecure defaults in programming languages (Python, Ruby, PHP, Perl...) or libraries, it is common for certificates to either be not verified at all or only have the trust chain verified. Often the very important check to see if the hostname matches the certificate doesn't happen. This type of fault can persist if it isn't detected before launch as developers are loath to make changes port-launch that may break the existing code.

- Because proper certificate checking is often a pain point during development and seriously gets in the way of testing, lots of iOS- and Android developers explicitly disable certificate verification checking and then fail to enable the checks in production versions.

- Lots of applications don't have proper hostname checks, i.e. they accept wildcards anywhere or multiple wildcards or even check the subject against a regex instead of a full DNS query.

Several programming languages like Python, PHP, Ruby, Perl and probably some others have recently moved or in the process of moving to proper verification of TLS by default. However, proper validation could have some undesirable consequences that will affect live code which implicitly expects no verification. There will therefore be a requirement to fix the code to expect proper TLS verification. Only as a last resort and only if these are just test scripts which don't work with sensitive data should TLS verification be disabled.

Hence the need to ensure that the application that we develop are build to support and leverage SSL/TLS and not to circumvent it as is too often the case.

However, there is a problem though with SSL in that it is all down to trust in the CA certification and diligent verification process and trust can be easily exploited. This is due to the fact that there are now 100's of CAs around the world so it doesn't really mean that an SSL certificate handled out by a CA is actually a genuine certificate. You see way back in 2011, a CA company issued legitimate certificates for Google, Skype, and many more thinking that they were genuine requests albeit the FQDNs were very similar. The problem was they were not genuine requests but carefully manipulated domain names that appeared to automated processes to be unique domains despite looking identical to Google and others, to the human eye! The trick was to use weird character set symbols that looked uncannily like ASCII characters to construct a domain name and of course to a machine there was no similarity. Now, here lies the problem, if the trusted CA could be so easily fooled then we really have a problem.

Indeed the trusted entities whose job it was to verify domain owners at the very least, and ideally also verify the business owners were genuine, instead appeared to be somewhat less than diligent. Hence, some SSL CAs were, back in 2011, issuing domain certificates to another nation who had applied and were duly supplied, despite having foreign IP addresses, with authenticated certificates for major internet entities, Google, Skype, Yahoo, and many more.

This is truly astonishing, that no one would check, after all this is the basis of the trust chain, and the foundations of internet security.

Furthermore, SSL has other problems. You see the SSL verification process actually does state when and how a client browser should check the certificate, for relevance, validity, and that it is genuine. But that is all SSL specifies as X.509 certificates are not part of the SSL/TLS standard or specification. This is because digital certificates are just one of several methods and ways that SSL/TLS can use to authenticate the identity of the other party.

Consequently, the standard for verification of the SSL certificate comes down to the X.509 specifications. As a result, a browser does not check that the certificate is actually owned by the business, as it has nothing to compare it with. Therefore as far as the browser is concerned if the certificate it receives exists in its vault or importantly if an intermediate CA certificate exists then fine it is okay.

What happens here is that a rouge site could respond with a fake certificate, because a man-in-the-middle attack can send back a fake certificate with the correct domain name and CA chain which will fool the browser into thinking that it is the genuine website.

Consequently we need to address the question of SSL certificate pinning within our applications.

SSL Pinning in iOS and Android

The default way an SSL connections work is as follows. The client makes a connection to the server and the server responds with its SSL certificate. If that certificate was issued by a Certificate Authority that is trusted by the OS, then the connection is allowed. All data sent through this connection is then encrypted with the server's public key. The part that is of interest to us is "trust." For an attacker to perform a "man in the middle" attack, the mobile device would have to trust the attacker's certificate. It is very unlikely that the attacker possesses a trusted certificate and therefore this is normally not an issue. However SSL weaknesses have happened before and using SSL Pinning can mitigate this possibility. Your app has the ability to use SSL Pinning to avoid this type of snooping.

SSL Pinning is making sure the client checks the server's certificate against a known copy of that certificate. Simply bundle your server's SSL certificate inside your application, and make sure any SSL request first validates that the server's certificate EXACTLY matches the bundle's certificate.

The method to do this in iOS is to add the certificate within:

```
connection:willSendRequestForAuthenticationChallenge:
```

inside the NSURLConnectionDelegate protocol. This method gets called when an SSL connection is made, giving you, the programmer, a chance to inspect the authentication challenge and either proceed or fail.

```
- (void)connection:(NSURLConnection *)connection
willSendRequestForAuthenticationChallenge:(NSURLAuthenticationChallenge
*)challenge
{
SecTrustRef serverTrust = challenge.protectionSpace.serverTrust;
SecCertificateRef certificate = SecTrustGetCertificateAtIndex(serverTrust, 0);
NSData *remoteCertificateData =
CFBridgingRelease(SecCertificateCopyData(certificate));
NSString *cerPath = [[NSBundle mainBundle]
pathForResource:@"MyLocalCertificate" ofType:@"cer"];
NSData *localCertData = [NSData dataWithContentsOfFile:cerPath];
if ([remoteCertificateData isEqualToData:localCertData]) {
NSURLCredential *credential = [NSURLCredential
credentialForTrust:serverTrust];
[[challenge sender] useCredential:credential
forAuthenticationChallenge:challenge];
}
else {
[[challenge sender] cancelAuthenticationChallenge:challenge];
}
```

The code above shows how you can check the certificate sent by the server, with a known certificate embedded in your applications.

SSL Pinning in Android

In Android the method is different and you need to use Retrofit or a similar program to expose a class called to make the SSL pinning.

Implement pinning in Retrofit we need two things

1. Host to be verified

2. public key hash of the host

So as an example to implement pinning for **api.github.com,** we need its public key hash from the certificate. We can get its public key hash by using openssl command line tools.

```
openssl s_client -connect api.github.com:443 | openssl x509 -pubkey -
noout | openssl rsa -pubin -outform der | openssl dgst -sha256 -binary |
openssl enc -base64
```

The OpenSSL command will return the SHA256 hash of the public key. Now we need a way to expose a Java class called CertificatePinner, by configuring can bind the public key to the host.

```
CertificatePinner certificatePinner = new
CertificatePinner.Builder()
```

```
.add("api.github.com",

"sha256/6wJsqVDF8K19zxfLxV5DGRneLyzso9adVdUN/exDacw=")


.build();


final OkHttpClient client =

httpBuilder.certificatePinner(certificatePinner).build();



Retrofit retrofit = new

Retrofit.Builder()


.baseUrl(END_POINT)


.addConverterFactory(GsonConverterFactory.create())


.client(client)


.build()
```

Then attach the CertificatePinner to the OkHttpClient.

Unfortunately there is as you might have suspected a big drawback and
that is the certificate embedded in your app will eventually expire. Not
only that, some large web entities like Google change their certificates on

a regular basis i.e. they revolve around a few active certificates which will also break your app. Therefore, you are going to have to either a plan for an app update that contains an updated certificate, or code a way for the application to download the new certificate.

For some apps, SSL Pinning may be impossible to do. If your app allows users to enter in their own domain names to connect to services, then you have no opportunity to embed that certificate. However if your app is intended to connect to a known server, or set of servers, you have all the information you need to guarantee that client is indeed talking directly to the server and without a man in the middle eavesdropping.

Server mitigation against rogue certificates

As we have seen SSL/TLS is certainly not in invulnerable or my any means undefeatable and there are other reasons to take care as one of the biggest threats to SSL/TLS is open WiFI connections whereby another party can easily eavesdrop on the traffic and try to intercept the data stream in what is known as a 'Man-in-the-Middle' (MiTM) attack. If an attacker can intercept traffic for example in an open WiFi area then they can use a rogue certificate to trick the browser into thinking that its connected to the genuine server => this is the worst case and this is what we want to prevent.

On the other hand, we might consider, a rouge developer trying to 'mitm' their client's traffic by modifying their own App to harvest data and send it back to a hidden URL.

HTTP Public Key Pinning

The solution or at least a potential mitigation is to use a technique called HTTP Public Key Pinning. To explain how HPKP works we will take a look at an example in the wild. However it is not as clear cut as we might think, for example what do you pin too?

In February of 2014, security researchers at Praetorian announced that they discovered that WhatsApp, the popular texting and multi-media application bought by Facebook, was also not implementing HTTP Public Key pinning, and had thereby exposing its users to MiTM attacks.

"Without SSL pinning enforced, an attacker could man-in-the-middle the connection between the mobile applications and back-end web services. This would allow the attacker to sniff user credentials, session identifiers, or other sensitive information."

Although it is extremely difficult for a fraudster to obtain a certificate for a domain he does not control, it is not impossible. For example there is plenty of precedence of certificate authorities having lax issuance policies that may have been breached or otherwise compromised by attackers.

The solution is to use a technique called HPKP. This is a mechanism to limit the number of Certificate Authorities ("CAs") trusted to sign for a specified website. The HPKP header is motivated by the history of the miss-issue of SSL/TLS certificates and the goal is to mitigate fraudulent use of otherwise valid certificates.

Enter PUBLIC KEY PINNING, which is a technique that enables site owners to have a say in which certificates are valid for their sites. For example, website owners select a set of public keys that must be used in future connections. When a client's browser visits the site, an HPKP policy is passed down to it via the HTTP Response Header that contains amongst other things the public keys/certificates that the site owner wishes them to validate against on subsequent visits. The client browser stores these certificates in its repository and obediently rejects any future connections to the sites servers that offer different public keys. By providing the browser with examples to check against the web site can ensure that only the genuinely held site certificates will be validated any other miss-issued but valid certificates will be rejected.

Public key pinning started at Google, when they started by pinning their own web site certificates in their proprietary web browser Chrome. Their approach is an example of STATIC PINNING; the pins are not easy to change because they're embedded in the browser. Moreover, Google also encouraged that other organisations embed their pins in Chrome and these days Firefox also supports static pinning. Google's Chrome browser's pinning of websites has worked well over the years, and has detected many cases of fraudulent certificates that would otherwise perhaps have gone unnoticed.

Whereas static pinning works well, it unfortunately just doesn't scale because maintaining pins is a slow manual process. For that reason Google launched an initiative with the IETF to develop a standard known as "Public Key Pinning Extension for HTTP", but which everybody calls just

HPKP. HPKP is an example of DYNAMIC PINNING as web site owners can set the pins at will.

Supporting dynamic pinning is very important as the trust chain can grow exponentially. Hence HPKP's design goal is to limit ("pin") a trusted list of server certificates locally so a client does not have to confer trust to any of the hundreds of CAs in the world. The result is that the HPKP browser can then pin a server's certificate immediately from its own repository or failing that call a limited set of CAs which were used to sign a server's certificate. At least one of the public keys of the certificates in the certificate chain needs to match a pinned public key in order for the chain to be considered valid by the user agent. A very beneficial side-effect of SSL Pinning is that it greatly reduces latency and improves efficiency thereby freeing up inefficiently consumed resources.

The way that HPKP works is that the server communicates the HPKP policy to the user agent via an HTTP response header field named Public-Key-Pins. The HPKP policy in the header contains hashes of one of the CA certificates in the website's authentic X.509 public key certificate chain and at least one backup key in pin-sha256 directives. Also contained within the HPKP policy is a max-age, which is a designated period of time during which the user agent shall enforce public key pinning. Optionally there is the directive in pinning policy to include all sub domains of the base domain that sent the header. Another optional switch is to send pinning violation reports via a report-uri directive.

There are three types of key that can be pinned using HPKP:

- The current public key of the certificate issued to a site.

- Public keys corresponding to certificate authorities and their intermediate certificates.

- Backup keys.

In order for browsers to accept and store a website's HPKP policy, there must be at least two pins specified in the HPKP policy. At least one pin must be in the chain of trust formed by the browser when verifying the site's certificate, and there must be at least one pin that is *not* in the chain (a *backup* pin).

At least one backup key must be pinned, in case the current pinned key needs to be replaced. The HPKP is not valid without this backup key (a backup key is defined as a public key not present in the current certificate chain).

HPKP is a dynamic expansion on static certificate pinning, which is limited by scalability due to the hard-coding of the public key hashes of well-known websites or services within web browsers and applications. Furthermore, dynamic pinning mitigates having to recode applications that have certificates that are due to expire or have for whatever reason a need to be revoked. Furthermore, hashes for HPKP policy can be generated by shell commands making the entire process both dynamic, easy to administer and simple to operate.

So what could possibly go wrong?

Unfortunately there are a number of issues with HPKP in real world operations. The main problem with HPKP, and with pinning in general, is that in the wrong hands it can be very destructive. The issue is that once

HPKP is set, it remains valid for a period of time designated by the max-age period which is measured in months. Webmasters therefore must display some cautious when pinning certificate authority keys. CAs may change their issuance practices without notice, and new certificates may not use the same chain of trust as the old ones. If the new certificate chain no longer includes the pinned keys, the website will not be accessible until the HPKP policy expires –ouch!

To avoid the problems posed by using certificate authority keys, webmasters can elect to pin their own keys. This is also a risky practice if the backup key cannot be used: it may have been lost, or may no longer qualify for inclusion in certificates, but it's your public key so it is readily replaceable.

Now if that isn't scary, then this should certainly be for there is an even scarier and potentially bigger problem with HPKP and that is it can be very effectively abused by an attacker. Let's say, for example, that someone breaks into your server and thus gains control of your web site. They can then silently activate HPKP and serve pinning instructions to a large chunk of your user base. Then after a reconnaissance period they remove the pinning keys from the server and brick your web site. Similar to crypto attacks where Ransomware attackers encrypt your system these attackers if you're lucky they may seek a ransom in return for the backup pinning key.

There is some relief in the fact that a valid HPKP configuration must include at least one backup key. The idea is that, if you something goes seriously wrong, you fetch your securely-stored backup key and resume normal operation.

Even if you don't lose your pinning keys, you have to be careful how and when you're changing them. Your configuration must, at any time, be offering at least one pin that matches the configuration you offered to all your previous users. If you rotate the keys too quickly you risk not having a pin for some of your older visitors.

To sum up, HPKP is not for the faint of heart; you essentially need to know what you're doing and be careful about it.

Clearly, pinning introduces a major conundrum for system administrators. HPKP can prevent fraudsters using a flawed but otherwise valid TLS certificates and offers a robust defense against website impersonation. Despite this hardly any HTTPS websites less that 0.1% are actually making use of this powerful security feature, even though it has been supported by some browsers for more than a year. The problem is that HPKP is seen as a double edge sword if ever there was one, it's very enticing but awfully dangerous and if administrators are not confident regards their key management strategies then they are voting to give HPKP a wide berth for the present.

Talking about knowing what you're doing, HPKP is also too flexible about what you can do with it. With it you can pin any public key in the certificate chain, choosing from your own keys (the leaf certificate), the intermediate certificates, or the root. Each decision comes with its advantages and disadvantages, but you need to understand PKI very well to appreciate them. This flexibility is a point of great confusion that in practice often leads to paralysis ("What to do?"). Some sites will inevitably make the wrong choice and suffer for it.

Thus, a successful pinning strategy requires that you:

1. Build a threat model to determine if there is a real threat out there that pinning can address at an acceptable cost

2. Understand PKI and HPKP and choose the right place to pin

3. Avoid losing your pinning keys

4. Keep backup keys in a separate location in case of server compromise

5. Have a robust plan for the key rotation and execute it smoothly

HPKP is safe in careful diligent hands where there is good key management policy. However the deployment figures are so far disappointing especially when held in contrast with the deployed instances of HSTS in the same survey with only 0.09% of all certificates in Netcraft's March 2016 SSL Survey are using HPKP and that relates to fewer than 4,100 certificates in the whole world that are being delivered with the Public-Key-Pins header.

HTTP Strict Transport Security (HSTS)

The growth of HTTPS has been a very encouraging and from a security, privacy and commerce perspective a positive step in the evolution of the internet. Secure communications has enabled more users to trade with confidence with more secure websites than ever before. Indeed many high profile sites now use HTTPS by default, and millions of TLS certificates are currently in use on the web. Encrypted communications are an essential requirement for banks and other financial websites, but HTTPS alone is not sufficient to defend these sites against man-in-the-middle attacks. Despite this, many secure financial services and banking websites are amongst the 95% of HTTPS servers that lack HTTP Strict Transport Security (HSTS). The lack of this protocol renders them vulnerable to pharming and man-in-the-middle attacks and despite this fact only around 5% of secure servers currently makes use of HSTS even though it is widely supported by practically all modern browsers.

Each secure website that does NOT implement an HSTS policy is vulnerable to compromise through man-in-the-middle attacks on the HTTP connections. This is a common attack vector, as there are many ways in which a user can inadvertently end up connecting via HTTP instead of HTTPS and annoyingly it is easily circumvented.

HSTS is a web security policy mechanism which protects websites against protocol downgrade attacks, i.e. from HTTPS to HTTP and against pervasive cookie hijacking. Web administrators can configure their web servers to designate that web browsers should only interact with it using secure HTTPS connections, and never via the insecure HTTP protocol.

SSL-stripping man-in-the-middle attacks, first publicly introduced by Moxie Marlinspike in his 2009 BlackHat Federal talk "New Tricks for Defeating SSL in Practice" is one of the important vulnerabilities that HSTS can mitigate. The way that the SSL/TLS stripping attack works is by converting a secure HTTPS connection into a plain HTTP connection. Although the user can very often see that the connection has down-graded from HTTPS to being insecure HTTP, they crucially have no way of knowing whether the connection *should* be secure. As a result many websites do not use TLS/SSL throughout their sites. Some only utilize SSL/TLS on the sign in and landing pages but revert back to HTTP for other pages therefore there is no way of knowing if the site should be secured or not. Consequently, users carry on browsing regardless to whether the use of plain HTTP is simply because the website hasn't implemented TLS/SSL or it is an attack. Additionally, no warnings are presented to the user during the downgrade process, making the attack fairly subtle to all but the most vigilant, which face it is not a description that matches the average web user.

HSTS addresses this problem by informing the browser that connections to the site should always use TLS/SSL. However, it is not quite that easy as the HSTS header can be stripped by the attacker if this is the user's first visit to the web site. In Chrome, Firefox, and Microsoft Edge there have been attempts to limit this problem by including a "pre-loaded" list of HSTS sites. Unsurprisingly, this has limited effect as this solution cannot scale to include all websites on the internet.

The way that HSTS works is that a server implements an HSTS policy by supplying a header over an HTTPS connection. For example, a server could send a header such that future requests to the domain for the next year use only HTTPS: Strict-Transport-Security: max-age=31536000.

The max=age is the life span of the command and in this example it equates to one year. The other directives open to HSTS are the option to include all sub-domains of the base domain on the web server. In order to preload a list of clients Google maintains an HSTS preload service. Hence, by following the guidelines and successfully submitting your domain, browsers will never connect to your domain using an insecure connection. While the service is hosted by Google, all browsers have stated an intent to use (or actually started using) the preload list.

The problem is best witnessed when a web site accepts a connection through HTTP from a web client browser and then tries to redirect the client to use HTTPS. The web client in this scenario will initially connect over HTTP to the non-encrypted version of the site before being redirected. The security issue is that if the user could possibly be redirected to a malicious site instead of the secure version of the original page by a malicious attacker.

To mitigate the risk of this type of session hijack the HTTP Strict Transport Security header lets a web site inform the browser that it should never load the site using HTTP and should automatically convert all attempts to access the site using HTTP to HTTPS requests instead. The max-age setting in the header corresponds to the life-span of the HSTS Policy such that (max-age is specified in seconds; 31,536,000 is equal to one non-leap year).

An interesting caveat of the HSTS protocol is that is rather unintuitive in so much as the web server and client ignore HSTS header went sent over HTTP. Why this should be is that an attacker would be able to see the headers in the clear and possibly corrupt or delete the headers in transit. Consequently HSTS headers are only recognized by the client browser if it receives them over an HTTPS connection as then it is able to infer that the site is SSL/TLS capable and will therefore honor the Strict-Transport-Security header.

When a web application issues HSTS Policy to user agents, conformant user agents behave as follows:

1. Automatically turn any insecure links referencing the web application into secure links. (For instance, http://example.com/some/page/ will be modified to https://example.com/some/page/ *before* accessing the server.)

2. If the security of the connection cannot be ensured (e.g. the server's TLS certificate is not trusted), show an error message and do not allow the user to access the web application.

The HSTS Policy helps protect web application users against some passive (eavesdropping) and active network attacks. A man-in-the-middle attacker has a greatly reduced ability to intercept requests and responses between a user and a web application server while the user's browser has HSTS Policy in effect for that web application.

FIPS140-2

What is FIPS140-2?

In several industries in the US it is essential that companies comply with legislation that insists upon deploying the Federal Information Processing Standard 140-2 (FIPS 140-2), which is a U.S. and Canadian co-sponsored security standard for hardware, software, and firmware solutions. For example in U.S. government procurement, all solutions that use cryptography must complete FIPS 140-2 validation to ensure end users receive a high degree of security, assurance, and dependability.

Federal agencies using validated cryptographic modules to protect sensitive government data in computer and telecommunication systems must use products that have completed FIPS validation.

Importantly, it is essential to understand the difference between products that are FIPS 140-2 validated and ones that are claiming to be FIPS 140-2 compliant.

FIPS compliant is a self designated term and has no government backing and is sometimes used to describe a product that uses FIPS approved algorithms, guidelines or libraries, but has not actually gone through the necessary steps to verify and test that the product is using them correctly.

For example, you may come across the term FIPS Inside, which typically refers to a third party product that has incorporated another company's cryptographic module. Although the cryptographic module that is inside has indeed gone through validation process, the overall product still has not yet been validated.

FIPS Validated asserts that the specific solution has gone through the entire FIPS 140-2 process, and been awarded a certificate issued by NIST (the government). Further, it validates that the product has been tested and meets the legal requirements passed by Congress, as well as the procurement requirements for the U.S. government and different industries, including healthcare, financial services and critical infrastructure.

Consequently, if your business is with NIST or you operate in any of the critical areas of security such as healthcare, financial services and critical infrastructure then you need to be using FIPS 140-2 crypto-modules.

However, if your business has highly sensitive web applications you may be the target of determined attackers (a common threat model for Internet accessible applications handling sensitive data), so it is strongly advised to use TLS services that are provided by FIPS 140-2 validated cryptomodule.

A cryptomodule can be a software library or a hardware device, which has its own services, which are the web applications that call the cryptomodule and they also depend on the correct implementation and integration of each of the following three components:

- Cryptographic algorithms (symmetric and asymmetric algorithms, hash algorithms, random number generator algorithms, and message authentication code algorithms)

- Inputs and outputs, which include cryptographic keys and so-called critical security parameters that call and manage crypto functions

- A physical container around the components that implement cryptographic algorithms and the components that call and manage cryptographic functions

To ensure that the cryptomodule is implemented, used and accessed securely requires that the following have been taken into consideration:

- The secure calling and managing of cryptographic functions

- Securely Handling inputs and output

- Ensuring the secure construction of the physical container around the components

In order to leverage the benefits of TLS it is important to use a TLS service (e.g. library, web framework, web application server) which has been FIPS 140-2 validated. In addition, the cryptomodule must be installed, configured and operated in either an approved or an allowed mode to provide a high degree of certainty that the FIPS 140-2 validated cryptomodule is providing the expected security services in the expected manner.

If the system is legally required to use FIPS 140-2 encryption (e.g., owned or operated by or on behalf of the U.S. Government) then TLS must be used and SSL disabled.

NOTE: Furthermore, companies that are legally required to use FIPS 140-2 must ignore the following best practices and instead adhere to the specific instructions for implementing and operation their FIPS 140-2 Cryptomodule.

SSL/TLS Best Practice

SSL/TLS is a deceptively simple technology. It is easy to deploy, and it just works--except when it does not. The main problem is that encryption is not often easy to deploy CORRECTLY. To ensure that TLS provides the necessary security, system administrators and developers must put extra effort into properly configuring their servers and developing their applications.

In 2009, we began our work on SSL Labs because we wanted to understand how TLS was used and to remedy the lack of easy-to-use TLS tools and documentation. We have achieved some of our goals through our global surveys of TLS usage, as well as the online assessment tool, but the lack of documentation is still evident. This document is a step toward addressing that problem.

Our aim here is to provide clear and concise instructions to help overworked administrators and programmers spend the minimum time possible to deploy a secure site or web application. In pursuit of clarity, we sacrifice completeness, foregoing certain advanced topics. The focus is on advice that is practical and easy to follow. For those who want more information, Section 6 gives useful pointers.

1 Private Key and Certificate

In TLS, all security starts with the server's cryptographic identity; a strong private key is needed to prevent attackers from carrying out impersonation attacks. Equally important is to have a valid and strong certificate, which grants the private key the right to represent a particular hostname. Without these two fundamental building blocks, nothing else can be secure.

1.1 Use 2048-Bit Private Keys

The private key used to generate the cipher key must be sufficiently strong for the anticipated lifetime of the private key and corresponding certificate. The current best practice is to select a key size of at least 2048 bits. The RSA public key algorithm is widely supported on most web sites, which makes these types of keys a safe default choice. RSA provides about 112 bits of security from 2,048 bits keys. If you feel that you need more security than this, then RSA is probably not the best choice as it doesn't scale well. For example, to raise the security level to just 128 bits requires that you use RSA keys of 3,072-bits, which are much slower. Consequently you may want to look at ECDSA keys provide an alternative solution that offers better security, scalability and much more efficient and better performance. For example at ECDSA -256 bits, these keys provide 128 bits of security. Of course there is always a drawback and that is that a small number of older clients don't support ECDSA, but modern client browsers do.

1.2 Protect Private Keys

It is imperative that the private key must be stored in a location that is protected from unauthorized access. So make sure that you treat your private keys as an important asset, restricting access to the smallest possible group of trusted employees. Recommended policies for key management include some of the following:

- If you cannot generate the private keys on the computer the certificate will be served from always perform the task on a trusted computer preferable air locked and that is capable of producing sufficient randomness or entropy.

- Always password-protect keys to prevent compromise when they are stored in backup systems and always check and remove keys from servers that are being retired. Unfortunately, private key passwords will not help much in production because a knowledgeable attacker can always retrieve the keys from process memory. If you have sufficient budget and work in a high security location then consider using Hardware Security Modules, or HSMs, which are hardware appliances that can protect private keys even in the case of server compromise.

- After compromise, revoke old certificates and generate new keys.

- Renew certificates on an annual basis even though it might be very tempting to go for a 3 year stint but in practice it is almost impossible to really revoke a stolen, lost or otherwise compromised certificate so the shorter the certificate lifespan the better. You may even be able to find the time to automate the process to make it less stressful and painful.

- Ideally it is best practice to generate new private keys whenever you're getting a new certificate do not just renew the old keys – unfortunately that doesn't work well if you are using certificate pinning which is also recommended – but it is something to consider.

1.3 Ensure Sufficient Hostname Coverage

A user should never experience a certificate error when accessing the server, especially those unnecessary prompts to reconcile domain or hostname mismatches, or expired certificates. If the application is available at both https://www.example.com and https://example.com then there should be an appropriate certificate, or certificates. Preferably, each site should have its own dedicated certificate. The danger of using self signed or incorrect domain certificates is that the users will become desensitized to TLS error messages and be encouraged to ignore them, which is counter to all security awareness training – but it does happen. Also this will increases the possibility an attacker could launch a convincing phishing or man-in-the-middle attack in future.

Even when you expect to use only one domain name, remember that you cannot control how your users arrive at the site or how others link to it. In most cases, you should ensure that the certificate works with and without the WWW prefix (e.g., that it works for both EXAMPLE.COM and www.example.com). The rule of thumb is that a secure web server should have a certificate that is valid for every DNS name configured to point to it.

Alternatively, there are certificates designed for hosting multiple web sites on a single server and these Subject Alternate Names (SANs) can be used to provide a specific listing of multiple names where the certificate is valid. In the example above, the certificate could list the Subject's CN as *example.com*, and list two SANs: *abc.example.com* and *xyz.example.com*. These certificates are sometimes referred to as "multiple domain certificates".

SANs are good but do not use wildcard certificates. Some people do like to use wildcard certificates for internal use and they do have their uses. However, they also have their inherent risks as many domains are then likely to be supported and sometimes that can mean different support teams that then give them access to the underlying keys. Therefore wildcards should not be encouraged as the fewer people there are with access to the private keys, the better.

1.4 Obtain appropriate Certificates from a Reliable CA

For Internet accessible websites, it is essential to purchase the TLS certificate from a recognize certification authority. There should not be instances where application users receive errors that the CA is unrecognized. Indeed if the certificate is purchased from a recognized CA then all modern Internet browsers will already contain the public certificates of these recognized certification authorities.

Therefore it is best as the company's reputation is on the line to select a Certification Authority (CA) that is reliable and consciences about its certificate business and security. Most are but there have been instances where some have been more interested in sales than strict verification. Therefore it is always a best practice to show due diligence when selecting a CA and consider the following criteria:

Security posture - All CAs have to undergo regular audits, but some are more serious about security than others. Figuring out which ones are better in this respect is not easy, but one option is to examine their security history, and, more important, how they have reacted to compromises and if they have learned from their mistakes.

Business focus – Look to CAs who specialize in SSL certificates as a major part of their business as they are likely to be more diligent as this is an important business procedure for them so they are less likely to be negligent or careless.

Services offered It is important to go to a CA that provides the type of SSL certificates you require. Not all CAs provide the full range of certificates.

Some will only provide organizational and extended verification certificates and will not provide domain verified certificates. On the other hand many will provide only domain verified certificates and will not provide the more taxing organizational and extended validation certificates. No matter what certificate you go for you should also have a choice regards the type of key algorithm, most offer RSA as a first and only choice of public key algorithm. However, ECDSA is now becoming more important and will do so in the future because of its performance advantages.

Certificate management options If you need a large number of certificates and operate in a complex environment, choose a CA that will give you good tools to manage them.

Support Choose a CA that will give you good support if and when you need it.

Note

For best results, acquire your certificates well in advance and at least one week before deploying them to production. This practice (1) helps avoid certificate warnings for some users who don't have the correct time on their computers and (2) helps avoid failed revocation checks with CAs who need extra time to propagate new certificates as valid to their OCSP responders. Over time, try to extend this "warm-up" period to 1-3 months. Similarly, don't wait until your certificates are about to expire to replace them. Leaving an extra several months there would similarly help with people whose clocks are incorrect in the other direction.

1.6 Use Strong Certificate Signature Algorithms

Because of issues with SHA1 which was until recently the de facto standard hashing algorithm for digital signing of certificates and most certificates relied on the SHA1 hashing function, it is now considered insecure. As a result, the industry is currently in transition to SHA256. Consequently as of January 2016, you shouldn't be able to get a SHA1 certificate from a public CA. The existing SHA1 certificates will continue to work (with warnings in some browsers), but only until the end of 2016. Therefore it is important to ensure that all certificates obtained are now supporting SHA256 or similar and be aware of and have a plan for the depreciation of SHA-1 certificates.

As a result of the steady depreciation and sunsetting policy of SHA1 being carried out by major browser vendors – Google probably being the most aggressive. It is important to avoid presenting end users with certificate warnings about SHA1 therefore organizations must proactively address the browser vendor's upcoming SHA-1 deprecation plans.

1.7 Use Complete Certificate Chains

It is important to ensure that clients are not burdened with the problem of having to attempt to solve the identity of a server or host using X509 certificates. When a user receives a server or host's certificate, the certificate must be validated back to a trusted root certification authority. This is known as path validation.

The problem arises due the fact that there can be one or more intermediate certificates in between the end-entity (server or host) certificate and root certificate. In addition to validating both endpoints, the client will also have to validate all intermediate certificates. Validating all intermediate certificates can be tricky because the user may not have them locally. This is a well-known PKI issue called the "Which Directory?" problem. Consequently all intermediary certificates must be bundled with the public certificate so that the client has a path back to the root CA.

A common configuration problem occurs when deploying a server with a valid certificate, but without all the necessary intermediate certificates. Sometimes they might require to be concatenated and then uploading as a bundle of certificates to the server. To avoid this situation, simply use all the certificates provided to you by your CA and follow their instructions.

We want to avoid this where ever possible as an invalid certificate chain effectively renders the server certificate invalid and results in browser warnings. In practice, this problem is sometimes difficult to diagnose because some browsers are more robust that others and can reconstruct incomplete chains while others can't or won't.

2 Server Design

2.1 Use TLS where ever you can

All networks, both external and internal, must utilize TLS or an equivalent transport layer security mechanism for all communication, prior versions of SSL are no longer acceptable. It is not sufficient to claim that access to the internal network is private as a simple scan of network traffic within the LAN will almost always uncover suspicious traffic and unauthorized network tools being used by employees if not full breaches by attackers. In these attacks, sniffers have been installed to access unencrypted sensitive data sent on the internal network.

The login page and all subsequent authenticated pages must be exclusively accessed over TLS. The initial login page, referred to as the "login landing page", must be served over TLS. Failure to utilize TLS for authenticated pages after the login enables an attacker to view the unencrypted session ID and compromise the user's authenticated session. Therefore all pages and content should be served over a TLS connection not just the authentication pages.

All pages which are available over TLS must not be available over a non-TLS connection. A user may inadvertently bookmark or manually type a URL to a HTTP page (e.g. http://example.com/myaccount) within the authenticated portion of the application. If this request is processed by the application then the response, and any sensitive data, would be returned to the user over the clear text HTTP.

2.2 Do Not Mix TLS and Non-TLS Content

A page that is available over TLS must be comprised completely of content which is transmitted over TLS. The page must not contain any content that is transmitted over unencrypted HTTP. A user may inadvertently bookmark or manually type a URL to a HTTP page (e.g. http://example.com/myaccount) within the authenticated portion of the application. If this request is processed by the application then the response, and any sensitive data, would be returned to the user over the clear text HTTP.

An attacker could intercept any of the data transmitted over the unencrypted HTTP and inject malicious content into the user's page. This malicious content would be included in the page even if the overall page is served over TLS. In addition, an attacker could steal the user's session cookie that is transmitted with any non-TLS requests. This is possible if the cookie's 'secure' flag is not set. See the rule 'Use "Secure" Cookie Flag'

2.3 Use "Secure" Cookie Flag

The "Secure" flag must be set for all user cookies. Failure to use the "secure" flag enables an attacker to access the session cookie by tricking the user's browser into submitting a request to an unencrypted page on the site. This attack is possible even if the server is not configured to offer HTTP content since the attacker is monitoring the requests and does not care if the server responds with a 404 or doesn't respond at all.

2.4 Keep Sensitive Data Out of the URL

Sensitive data must not be transmitted via URL arguments. A more appropriate place is to store sensitive data in a server side repository or within the user's session. When using TLS the URL arguments and values are encrypted during transit. However, there are two methods that the URL arguments and values could be exposed.

1. The entire URL is cached within the local user's browser history. This may expose sensitive data to any other user of the workstation.

2. The entire URL is exposed if the user clicks on a link to another HTTPS site. This may expose sensitive data within the referral field to the third party site. This exposure occurs in most browsers and will only occur on transitions between two TLS sites.

For example, a user following a link on https://example.com which leads to https://someOtherexample.com would expose the full URL of https://example.com (including URL arguments) in the referral header (within most browsers). This would not be the case if the user followed a link on https://example.com to http://someHTTPexample.com

2.5 Prevent Caching of Sensitive Data

The TLS protocol provides confidentiality only for data in transit but it does not help with potential data leakage issues at the client or intermediary proxies. As a result, it is frequently prudent to instruct these nodes not to cache or persist sensitive data. One option is to add anticaching headers to relevant HTTP responses, (for example, "Cache-Control: no-cache, no-store" and "Expires: 0" for coverage of many modern browsers as of 2013). For compatibility with HTTP/1.0 (i.e., when user agents are really old or the webserver works around quirks by forcing HTTP/1.0) the response should also include the header "Pragma: no-cache".

2.6 Use HTTP Strict Transport Security

Use HSTS whenever possible as it will enforce client browsers to always request an HTTPS secure connection over SSL/TLS. Using HSTS helps ensure that clients will use the SSL/TLS protocols, which is a major advance in enforcing public security compliance.

2.7 Use Public Key Pinning

With correct TLS server configuration, you ensure that your credentials are properly presented to the site's visitors, that only secure cryptographic primitives are used, and that all known weaknesses are mitigated.

3 Secure Protocols & Ciphers

The strength of the encryption used within a TLS session is determined by the encryption cipher negotiated between the server and the browser. In order to ensure that only strong cryptographic ciphers are selected the server must be modified to disable the use of weak ciphers and to configure the ciphers in an adequate order. It is recommended to configure the server to only support strong ciphers and to use sufficiently large key sizes. In general, the following should be observed when selecting cipher suites:

3.1 Use Secure Protocols

There are five protocols in the SSL/TLS family: SSL v2, SSL v3, TLS v1.0, TLS v1.1, and TLS v1.2:

- SSL v2 is insecure and must not be used. This protocol version is so bad that it can be used to attack RSA keys and sites with the same name even if they are on an entirely different servers (the DROWN attack).

- SSL v3 is insecure when used with HTTP (the POODLE attack) and weak when used with other protocols. It's also obsolete and shouldn't be used.

- TLS v1.0 is also a legacy protocol that shouldn't be used, but it's typically still necessary in practice. Its major weakness (BEAST) has been mitigated in modern browsers, but other problems remain.

- TLS v1.1 and v1.2 are both without known security issues, but only v1.2 provides modern cryptographic algorithms.

TLS v1.2 should be your main protocol because it's the only version that offers modern authenticated encryption (also known as AEAD). If you don't support TLS v1.2 today, your security is lacking.

In order to support older clients, you may need to continue to support TLS v1.0 and TLS v1.1 for now. Certainly for older versions of browsers and smartphones such as Android ver4 you will need to continue to support TLS v1.0. However, you should have in place plans to retire TLS v1.0 in the near future and this is not really under your control especially if you are supporting an ecommerce site. For example, the PCI DSS standard will require all sites that accept credit card payments to remove support for TLS v1.0 by June 2018.

Work is currently under way to design TLS v1.3, with the aims to remove all obsolete and insecure features and to make improvements that will keep our communication secure in the following decades. Unfortunately with industry standards and specifications continents shift quicker.

3.2 Prefer Ephemeral Key Exchanges

For secure key exchange, public web sites typically have the choice between using the classic ephemeral Diffie-Hellman key exchange (DHE) or its elliptic curve variant, ECDHE. There are other key exchange algorithms, but they're generally insecure in one way or another. The RSA key exchange is still very popular, and secure but it doesn't provide forward secrecy so we should no longer consider it as a suitable method for key exchange.

Therefore we should always prefer Ephemeral key exchanges, which are based on Diffie-Hellman and use per-session, temporary keys during the initial SSL/TLS handshake. The real advantage to using Ephemeral key exchanges, which has captured the imagination of security professionals is that it provides perfect forward secrecy (PFS), which means a compromise of the server's long term signing key does not compromise the confidentiality of past session. Therefore, when the server uses an ephemeral key, the server will sign the temporary key with its long term key (the long term key is the customary key available in its certificate).

Despite the huge interest in DHE and EDHE it is not perfect by any means as in 2015, a group of researchers published new attacks against DHE; their work is known as the Logjam attack. What the researchers discovered was that at lower-strength (e.g., 768 bits) DH key exchanges could easily be compromised and then came the news that some well-known 1,024-bit DH groups could also be broken by state agencies. Hence, nowadays to be on the safe side, use cryptographic parameters (like DH-parameter) that use a secure length that match to the supported keylength of your certificate (>=2048 bits or equivalent Elliptic Curves). Do *not* use standardized DH-parameters as they they are defined by RFCs 2409, 3526, or 5114. Generate your own individual DH-parameters using the OPenSSL command line tools to get some unique prime numbers (this may take a long time): openssl dhparam 2048 -out dhparam2048.pem

3.3 Use Secure Cipher Suites

To communicate securely, you must first ascertain that you are communicating directly with the desired party (and not through someone else who will eavesdrop) and exchanging data securely. In SSL and TLS, cipher suites define how secure communication takes place. They are composed from varying building blocks with the idea of achieving security through diversity. If one of the building blocks is found to be weak or insecure, you should be able to switch to another.

You should rely chiefly on the AEAD suites that provide strong authentication and key exchange, forward secrecy, and encryption of at least 128 bits. Some other, weaker suites may still be supported, provided they are negotiated only with older clients that don't support anything better.

There are several obsolete cryptographic primitives that MUST be avoided:

- Anonymous Diffie-Hellman (ADH) suites do not provide authentication.

- NULL cipher suites provide no encryption.

- Export cipher suites are insecure when negotiated in a connection, but they can also be used against a server that prefers stronger suites (the FREAK attack).

- Suites with weak ciphers (typically of 40 and 56 bits) use encryption that can easily be broken.

- RC4 is insecure.

- 3DES is slow and weak.

3.4 Select Best Cipher Suites

In SSL v3 and later protocol versions, clients submit a list of cipher suites that they support, and servers choose one suite from the list to use for the connection. Not all servers do this well, however; some will select the first supported suite from the client's list. Having servers actively select the best available cipher suite is critical for achieving the best security.

3.5 Use Forward Secrecy

Forward secrecy (sometimes also called perfect forward secrecy) is a protocol feature that enables secure conversations that are not dependent on the server's private key. With cipher suites that do not provide forward secrecy, someone who can recover a server's private key can decrypt ALL earlier recorded encrypted conversations. You need to support and prefer ECDHE suites in order to enable forward secrecy with modern web browsers. To support a wider range of clients, you should also use DHE suites as fallback after ECDHE. Avoid the RSA key exchange unless absolutely necessary. My proposed default configuration in Section 2.3 contains only suites that provide forward secrecy.

3.6 Support TLS-PSK and TLS-SRP for Mutual Authentication

When using a shared secret or password offer TLS-PSK (Pre-Shared Key) or TLS-SRP (Secure Remote Password), which are known as Password Authenticated Key Exchange (PAKEs). TLS-PSK and TLS-SRP properly bind the channel, which refers to the cryptographic binding between the outer tunnel and the inner authentication protocol. IANA currently reserves 79 PSK cipher suites and 9 SRP cipher suites.

Basic authentication places the user's password on the wire in the plain text after a server authenticates itself. Basic authentication only provides unilateral authentication. In contrast, both TLS-PSK and TLS-SRP provide mutual authentication, meaning each party proves it knows the password without placing the password on the wire in the plain text.

Finally, using a PAKE removes the need to trust an outside party, such as a Certification Authority (CA).

3.7 Only Support Secure Renegotiations

A design weakness in TLS, identified as CVE-2009-3555, allows an attacker to inject a plaintext of his choice into a TLS session of a victim. In the HTTPS context the attacker might be able to inject his own HTTP requests on behalf of the victim. The issue can be mitigated either by disabling support for TLS renegotiations or by supporting only renegotiations compliant with RFC 5746. All modern browsers have been updated to comply with this RFC.

3.8 - Disable Compression

Compression Ratio Info-leak Made Easy (CRIME) is an exploit against the data compression scheme used by the TLS and SPDY protocols. The exploit allows an adversary to recover user authentication cookies from HTTPS. The recovered cookie can be subsequently used for session hijacking attacks.

4 Performance

Security is our main focus in this guide, but we must also pay attention to performance; a secure service that does not satisfy performance criteria will no doubt be dropped. With proper configuration, TLS can be quite fast. With modern protocols—for example, HTTP/2—it might even be faster than plaintext communication.

4.1 Avoid Too Much Security

The cryptographic handshake, which is used to establish secure connections, is an operation for which the cost is highly influenced by private key size. Using a key that is too short is insecure, but using a key that is too long will result in "too much" security and slow operation. For most web sites, using RSA keys stronger than 2,048 bits and ECDSA keys stronger than 256 bits is a waste of CPU power and might impair user experience. Similarly, there is little benefit to increasing the strength of the ephemeral key exchange beyond 2,048 bits for DHE and 256 bits for ECDHE. There are no clear benefits of using encryption above 128 bits.

4.2 Use Session Resumption

Session resumption is a performance-optimization technique that makes it possible to save the results of costly cryptographic operations and to reuse them for a period of time. A disabled or nonfunctional session resumption mechanism may introduce a significant performance penalty.

4.3 Use WAN Optimization and HTTP/2

These days, TLS overhead doesn't come from CPU-hungry cryptographic operations, but from network latency. A TLS handshake, which can start only after the TCP handshake completes, requires a further exchange of packets and is more expensive the further away you are from the server. The best way to minimize latency is to avoid creating new connections—in other words, to keep existing connections open for a long time (keep-alives). Other techniques that provide good results include supporting modern protocols such as HTTP/2 and using WAN optimization (usually via content delivery networks).

4.4 Cache Public Content

When communicating over TLS, browsers might assume that all traffic is sensitive. They will typically use the memory to cache certain resources, but once you close the browser, all the content may be lost. To gain a performance boost and enable long-term caching of some resources, mark public resources (e.g., images) as public.

4.5 Use OCSP Stapling

OCSP stapling is an extension of the OCSP protocol that delivers revocation information as part of the TLS handshake, directly from the server. As a result, the client does not need to contact OCSP servers for out-of-band validation and the overall TLS connection time is significantly reduced. OCSP stapling is an important optimization technique, but you should be aware that not all web servers provide solid OCSP stapling implementations. Combined with a CA that has a slow or unreliable OCSP responder, such web servers might create performance issues. For best results, simulate failure conditions to see if they might impact your availability.

4.6 Use Fast Cryptographic Primitives

In addition to providing the best security, my recommended cipher suite configuration also provides the best performance. Whenever possible, use CPUs that support hardware-accelerated AES. After that, if you really want a further performance edge (probably not needed for most sites), consider using ECDSA keys.

5 HTTP and Application Security

The HTTP protocol and the surrounding platform for web application delivery continued to evolve rapidly after SSL was born. As a result of that evolution, the platform now contains features that can be used to defeat encryption. In this section, we list those features, along with ways to use them securely.

5.1 Encrypt Everything

The fact that encryption is optional is probably one of the biggest security problems today. We see the following problems:

- No TLS on sites that need it

- Sites that have TLS but that do not enforce it

- Sites that mix TLS and non-TLS content, sometimes even within the same page

- Sites with programming errors that subvert TLS

Although many of these problems can be mitigated if you know exactly what you're doing, the only way to reliably protect web site communication is to enforce encryption throughout—without exception.

5.2 Eliminate Mixed Content

Mixed-content pages are those that are transmitted over TLS but include resources (e.g., JavaScript files, images, CSS files) that are not transmitted over TLS. Such pages are not secure. An active man-in-the-middle (MITM) attacker can piggyback on a single unprotected JavaScript resource, for example, and hijack the entire user session. Even if you follow the advice from the previous section and encrypt your entire web site, you might still end up retrieving some resources unencrypted from third-party web sites.

5.3 Understand and Acknowledge Third-Party Trust

Web sites often use third-party services activated via JavaScript code downloaded from another server. A good example of such a service is Google Analytics, which is used on large parts of the Web. Such inclusion of third-party code creates an implicit trust connection that effectively gives the other party full control over your web site. The third party may not be malicious, but large providers of such services are increasingly seen as targets. The reasoning is simple: if a large provider is compromised, the attacker is automatically given access to all the sites that depend on the service.

If you follow the advice from Section 4.2, at least your third-party links will be encrypted and thus safe from MITM attacks. However, you should go a step further than that: learn what services you use and remove them, replace them with safer alternatives, or accept the risk of their continued use. A new technology called sub-resource integrity (SRI) could be used to reduce the potential exposure via third-party resources.[3]

5.4 Secure Cookies

To be properly secure, a web site requires TLS, but also that all its cookies are explicitly marked as secure when they are created. Failure to secure the cookies makes it possible for an active MITM attacker to tease some information out through clever tricks, even on web sites that are 100% encrypted. For best results, consider adding cryptographic integrity validation or even encryption to your cookies.

5.5 Secure HTTP Compression

The 2012 CRIME attack showed that TLS compression can't be implemented securely. The only solution was to disable TLS compression altogether. The following year, two further attack variations followed. TIME and BREACH focused on secrets in HTTP response bodies compressed using HTTP compression. Unlike TLS compression, HTTP compression is a necessity and can't be turned off. Thus, to address these attacks, changes to application code need to be made.[4]

TIME and BREACH attacks are not easy to carry out, but if someone is motivated enough to use them, the impact is roughly equivalent to a successful Cross-Site Request Forgery (CSRF) attack.

5.6 Deploy HTTP Strict Transport Security

HTTP Strict Transport Security (HSTS) is a safety net for TLS. It was designed to ensure that security remains intact even in the case of configuration problems and implementation errors. To activate HSTS protection, you add a new response header to your web sites. After that, browsers that support HSTS (all modern browsers at this time) enforce it.

The goal of HSTS is simple: after activation, it does not allow any insecure communication with the web site that uses it. It achieves this goal by automatically converting all plaintext links to secure ones. As a bonus, it also disables click-through certificate warnings. (Certificate warnings are an indicator of an active MITM attack. Studies have shown that most users click through these warnings, so it is in your best interest to never allow them.)

Adding support for HSTS is the single most important improvement you can make for the TLS security of your web sites. New sites should always be designed with HSTS in mind and the old sites converted to support it wherever possible and as soon as possible. For best security, consider using HSTS preloading, which embeds your HSTS configuration in modern browsers, making even the first connection to your site secure.

The following configuration example activates HSTS on the main hostname and all its subdomains for a period of one year, while also allowing preloading:

Strict-Transport-Security: max-age=31536000; includeSubDomains; preload

5.7 Deploy Content Security Policy

Content Security Policy (CSP) is a security mechanism that web sites can use to restrict browser operation. Although initially designed to address Cross-Site Scripting (XSS), CSP is constantly evolving and supports features that are useful for enhancing TLS security. In particular, it can be used to restrict mixed content when it comes to third-party web sites, for which HSTS doesn't help.

To deploy CSP to prevent third-party mixed content, use the following configuration:

Content-Security-Policy: default-src https: 'unsafe-inline' 'unsafe-eval';
            connect-src https: wss:

Note

This is not the best way to deploy CSP. In order to provide an example that doesn't break anything except mixed content, I had to disable some of the default security features. Over time, as you learn more about CSP, you should change your policy to bring them back.

5.8 Do Not Cache Sensitive Content

All sensitive content must be communicated only to the intended parties and treated accordingly by all devices. Although proxies do not see encrypted traffic and cannot share content among users, the use of cloud-based application delivery platforms is increasing, which is why you need to be very careful when specifying what is public and what is not.

5.9 Consider Other Threats

TLS is designed to address only one aspect of security—confidentiality and integrity of the communication between you and your users—but there are many other threats that you need to deal with. In most cases, that means ensuring that your web site does not have other weaknesses.

6 Validation

With many configuration parameters available for tweaking, it is difficult to know in advance what impact certain changes will have. Further, changes are sometimes made accidentally; software upgrades can introduce changes silently. For that reason, we advise that you use a comprehensive SSL/TLS assessment tool initially to verify your configuration to ensure that you start out secure, and then periodically to ensure that you stay secure. For public web sites, we recommend the free SSL Labs server test.[6]

7 Advanced Topics

The following advanced topics are currently outside the scope of our guide. They require a deeper understanding of SSL/TLS and Public Key Infrastructure (PKI), and they are still being debated by experts.

7.1 Public Key Pinning

Public key pinning is designed to give web site operators the means to restrict which CAs can issue certificates for their web sites. This feature has been deployed by Google for some time now (hardcoded into their browser, Chrome) and has proven to be very useful in preventing attacks and making the public aware of them. In 2014, Firefox also added support for hardcoded pinning. A standard called Public Key Pinning Extension for HTTP[7] is now available. Public key pinning addresses the biggest weakness of PKI (the fact that any CA can issue a certificate for any web site), but it comes at a cost; deploying requires significant effort and expertise, and creates risk of losing control of your site (if you end up with invalid pinning configuration). You should consider pinning largely only if you're managing a site that might be realistically attacked via a fraudulent certificate.

7.2 DNSSEC and DANE

Domain Name System Security Extensions (DNSSEC) is a set of technologies that add integrity to the domain name system. Today, an active network attacker can easily hijack any DNS request and forge arbitrary responses. With DNSSEC, all responses can be cryptographically tracked back to the DNS root. DNS-based Authentication of Named Entities (DANE) is a separate standard that builds on top of DNSSEC to provide bindings between DNS and TLS. DANE could be used to augment the security of the existing CA-based PKI ecosystem or bypass it altogether.

Even though not everyone agrees that DNSSEC is a good direction for the Internet, support for it continues to improve. Browsers don't yet support either DNSSEC or DANE (preferring similar features provided by HSTS and HPKP instead), but there is some indication that they are starting to be used to improve the security of email delivery.

Implement and Configure SSL to Ward off Vulnerability

The ways to remediate SSL problems are to consider:

• Don't create more vulnerability by performing SSL traffic interception with a centralized network proxy. If you are filtering all your SSL traffic through a centralized network proxy, that proxy becomes a huge target for hackers and a goldmine if they're able to breach it.
• Implement a solution that allows you to gain visibility and control over web usage, on and off the corporate network, by performing on-device

analysis prior to SSL encryption.

• Protect sensitive data by default with an end-to-end encryption solution so that you do not have to inspect SSL traffic for potential data exfiltration. In this scenario, the sensitive data is always encrypted and access can be revoked if it leaves the enterprise without authorization.

Troubleshooting SSL/TLS

SSL/TLS is a wonderfully complex protocol that has been refined over the years into a module or package that is pre-installed in many instances and just works with little or no required heavy lifting. Except of course, when it doesn't.

Then we need to start the sometimes confusing and onerous task of troubleshooting what is actually going on during the SSL/TLS handshakes. Thankfully, everything up until the session is established is carried out in the clear so until communication are finally encrypted once the handshake is virtually completed we can monitor and observe what is going on using some standard tools open source or free tools such as Wireshark or Network Monitor.

For the vast majority of the time troubleshooting concerns the handshake as this is when both parties setup the session agree on a cipher suite, exchange keys and generate the shared secret key for the symmetric encryption for that session. Once the handshake is completed an SSL/TLS tunnel is setup and traffic can flow securely so is deemed to be working. If however you still have problems then you will need to analyse the encrypted traffic using tools such as sslsniff or ssldump – of course you will also need the keys.

However there are many tools already to hand or online that can assist you in many initial troubleshooting steps so let us take a look at some of the most helpful.

First and foremost if you are using OpenSSL which most will be there are the OpenSSL command line tools which can be used for initial verification and confirmation that the basic certificate and base configuration are OK. In order to test the basic installation and verify the certificate you can run these commands.

To manually verify a certificate and the keys match, which you should do at installation but can also check during troubleshooting use the command:

```
$ (openssl x509 -noout -modulus \
        -in /etc/apache2/ssl.crt/www.mysite.org.crt | openssl md5 ;\
    openssl rsa  -noout -modulus
        -in /etc/apache2/ssl.key/www.mysite.org.key | openssl md5) \
    | uniq
```

To verify a certificate use the command:

```
$ openssl verify -CAfile ca.crt www.mysite.org.crt
```

Once you have verified the certificate you will also want to verify your
intermediate CA-chain is complete using the OpenSSL command:

```
$ openssl verify -verbose cert-your_domain.pem
```

This will list the CAs in the chain and let you know if any links in the chain
are broken or out of order. For example should you get an error in the CA
listing such as:

error 20 at 0 depth lookup:unable to get local issuer certificate

Then that means OpenSSL has encountered a problem at depth 2 – the
third CA in the chain – and is unable to locate its root certificate.

Before we go any further we need to make sure that OpenSSL is logging
error correctly so check that the configuration is logging events in the
follow location:

```
<IfModule mod_ssl.c>
   ErrorLog /var/log/apache2/ssl_engine.log
   LogLevel debug
 </IfModule>
```

The type of logging information we will find in
/var/log/apache2/ssl_engine.log relate to significant SSL event such as
issues with session startup such as:

```
[Thu Jan 15 08:19:01 2016] [debug] ssl_engine_kernel.c(1791): OpenSSL:
Exit: error in SSLv3 read client certificate B
[Thu Jan 15 08:19:01 2016] [error] Re-negotiation handshake failed: Not
```

accepted by client!?

In the snippet from the SSL logs we can see that the client refused the connection – perhaps as it was SSL v3.0 – but for whatever reason it wasn't happy with the negotiated terms and we have a connection problem.

To check if a site supports the SSL/TLS protocols you can try a connection using OpenSSL command:

```
$ openssl s_client -ssl3 -connect your_server.com:443
```

If you are experiencing SSL handshake errors it is most likely down to certificate errors as they are very common. So lets us start with some tools and techniques for capturing and analyzing public certificates. Of course if there is a problem with the certificate the handshake is going to cause the connection attempt to fail.

Consequently, when troubleshooting general connection failures for example with the SSL/TLS handshake the first step
 is to check our connection using another OpenSSL command:

```
openssl s_client -showcerts -connect www.microsoft.com:443
```

**Note press Ctrl-C to quit the open connection.

This command will check if we can make a secure connection via a handshake to a server at www.microsoft.com and it will display the certificate chain if you don't want to see all the chain then just remove the –showcerts switch and then you will only get the server certificate.

If you see these errors:

error:num=21:unable to verify the first certificate

If you see this when you run this command, it means exactly what it says ... that chain of trust is broken right from the start. Typically it might happen if you fail to include intermediate certificates, or if you supply the wrong intermediate certificate.

Or

error:num=20:unable to get local issuer certificate

What this error means is that OpenSSL was unable to find a certificate for the issuer of a certificate it will usually provide additional information such as the depth in the chain '0,1,2 ...' and the CN of the CA. This is typically because the issuer is a root certificate and openSSL does not know where the root certificates are stored. This can be fixed by adding the -CAfile option pointing to a file containing all the trusted root certificates.

Sometimes it might be useful to decode a certificate in PEM or DER format the certs are decodes in weak Base64 so if you cut & paste the output from the screen to a file – including the Begin and end lines for PEM, the DER format doesn't have a begin– OpenSSL can decrypt the certificate for you.

| openssl x509 -noout -text -in cert-microsoft.pem |
| openssl x509 -noout -text -inform der -in cert_symantec.der |

The decoded certificate will look something like this:

| MBP$ openssl x509 -noout -text -in cert-microsoft.pem |
| Certificate: |

Data:

Version: 3 (0x2)

Serial Number:

35:f3:01:36:00:01:00:00:7e:2f

Signature Algorithm: sha1WithRSAEncryption

Issuer: DC=com, DC=microsoft, DC=corp, DC=redmond,

CN=MSIT Machine Auth CA 2

Validity

Not Before: Jun 20 20:29:28 2013 GMT

Not After : Jun 20 20:29:28 2015 GMT

Subject: CN=microsoft.com

Subject Public Key Info:

Public Key Algorithm: rsaEncryption

RSA Public Key: (2048 bit)

Modulus (2048 bit):

[removed for brevity]

Exponent: 65537 (0x10001)

X509v3 extensions:

X509v3 Subject Key Identifier:

89:28:65:2A:A9:12:FB:E5:33:9F:00:70:68:85:3E:

48:DD:6A:B8:C9

X509v3 Key Usage:

Digital Signature, Key Encipherment, Data

Encipherment

X509v3 Authority Key Identifier:

keyid:EB:DB:11:5E:F8:09:9E:D8:D6:62:9C:FD:

62:9D:E3:84:4A:28:E1:27

X509v3 CRL Distribution Points:

    URI:http://mscrl.microsoft.com/pki/mscorp/crl/

      MSIT%20Machine%20Auth%20CA%202(1).crl

    URI:http://crl.microsoft.com/pki/mscorp/crl/

      MSIT%20Machine%20Auth%20CA%202(1).crl

    URI:http://corppki/crl/MSIT%20Machine%20Auth%20

      CA%202(1).crl

Authority Information Access:

    CA Issuers - URI:http://www.microsoft.com/pki/

      mscorp/MSIT%20Machine%20Auth%20CA%202(1).crt

    CA Issuers - URI:http://corppki/aia/MSIT%20Machine

      %20Auth%20CA%202(1).crt

1.3.6.1.4.1.311.21.7:

    00.(+.....7.....M..........}...t.O.........c..d..

X509v3 Extended Key Usage:

    TLS Web Client Authentication, TLS Web Server

    Authentication

1.3.6.1.4.1.311.21.10:

    0.0

..+.......0

..+.......

```
Signature Algorithm: sha1WithRSAEncryption

[removed for brevity]
```

So now that we have the tools and know how to use them to acquire and analyse public certificate what problems are we likely to come across?

The most common problems with SSL certificates come about due to:

- Certificate and private key mismatch

  - Commonly the result of either no private key being present in the designated directory or it is the wrong key – check the file locations and verify the key
  - Verify that the CSR and key were generated on that server – if not locate the missing private key

- No intermediate certificates for CA chain

  - This is commonly the result of the intermediate certificates not being loaded to the server along with the SSL certificate – check they have been bundled correctly and served to the client along with the server/site certificate
  - Incorrect concatenation order of certificates in SSL cert bundle – check the servers public key is foremost in the queue

- Self-signed certificates. In this case there is no trust authority that can be checked for a local trust anchor and thus the certificate cannot be trusted. Browsers will flag this to the user's attention and some will allow the user to explicitly trust the certificate. If the certificate is loaded manually into the browsers SSL repository then many will explicitly trust the certificate.

- Certificate content does not match hostname. There are clear rules how the checks should be done, but some applications are less strict and others do not implement the checks correctly:

    o Private IP addressing is no longer allowed as of October 2016

    o Wildcards are only allowed in Subject Alternative Names section.

    o If a SAN section contains entries of type DNS then commonName should not be checked. Most browsers currently check commonName as well

- Certificate expired or not yet valid
    o Common if static certificate pinning is used within applications
- Clock mismatch between client and server
    o Lack of internet time protocol synchronization can mean clients erroneously think valid certificates have expired or are not yet valid
    o PC client/Server bios resets during OS fault recovery can reset clock back to 2000
- Server or client is unable to support Server Name Indication (SNI)

- Use 'openssl s_client' with and without '-servername' option. If the returned certificates differ then SNI is required. Some servers even fail completely when accessed without SNI.

- SSLLabs will also tell you if the site requires SNI ("This site works only in browsers with SNI support")

- Valid certificate fails verification
  - A common issue can be if SSL interception occurs inside a company as this will cause the CA certificate to be signed by a proxy CA. Verification will fail if this CA is not trusted by the application.
  - Verification might even fail in case of SSL interception if the proxy CA is trusted, because the application uses certificate/public key pinning.
  - The certificates Root-CA might be known on the system, but may not in the trust store used by the specific application.
- No shared cipher suites negotiated

  - Check that the supported cipher suites are compatible between client and server. A common problem is that SSL v3.0 ciphers have been disabled instead of disabling the protocol but the ciphers are still required by TLS.
  - Server is using old or export only ciphers which are no longer supported by client

- o No certificates are configured at the server, which then falls back to anonymous authentication. These ciphers are not supported by most clients for security reasons for example man-in-the-middle style attacks.

- Unexpected or missing public key/cert issued to a HPKP client from a HPKP server
  - o Ensure that the pinned certificate is being served to the client
- Not enough entropy to create CSR
  - o This is quite rare but confusing error that occurs when creating the CSR. As part of CSR generation is creating the private key the machine needs to have sufficient randomness or entropy in order to generate pseudo random numbers. Because headless servers without peripherals have low entropy pools this message can occur. The solution in Linux is always ensure that you stipulate to use the /dev/urandom in the config for entropy and NOT /dev/random

In all these cases either the certificate need to be fixed or the application or client must import the certificate as trusted or use certificate/public key pinning.

In many instances the first step in troubleshooting after confirmation that the basic SSL/TLS certificate config is OK is to use the divide and conquer method to find out what has gone wrong. Therefore, as there are two parties negotiating the SSL/TLS session it can be helpful to find out which one is experiencing the problem.

Therefore a good basic strategy is to narrow down the problem to the client or the server or something in between, i.e.

- Try to access the same server from different clients and browsers as this can be a common problem with mobile apps especially with Android 4.0 and below

- Try to access the same server from different networks after all firewalls, routing issues can all play their part in preventing a connection. If possible access the SSL server from the local host or at least from the servers local network as this rules out any networking issues

- Try to access different servers from the same client to verify if the client is working okay.

The quickest way to do this is if the machines are accessible from the internet and are public facing is to test out both the client browser and the server independently using an online tool which will analyse the SSL/TLS configuration respectively. A good tool for testing both the server and client functions is Qualsys SSL Labs
https://www.ssllabs.com/ssltest/analyze.html

SSL Labs will run tests to verify the functionality of both a client and a server for example here are some sample outputs from the basic online tests.

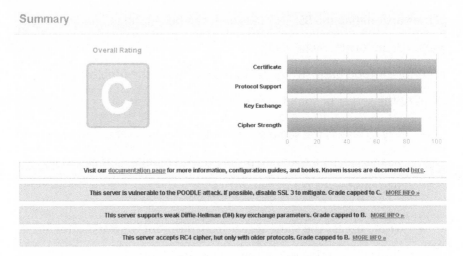

Summary

In addition the SSL Labs project will run tests to retrieve and decrypt the public certificate, list the supported protocols, cipher-suites and perform an array of handshake simulations with many clients, browsers and OS as well as provide a detailed breakdown of the protocol configurations, vulnerabilities and suggest remedial tasks.

Therefore for most public facing SSL servers and clients SSL Labs is a very convenient and simple first place to start any investigations.

If however as is often the case the SSL server is private and behind a firewall then you will have to use the traditional methods.

The following are some quick checks that you can perform to verify some common issues.

- How to check for missing intermediate CA certificates in a chain

- SSLLabs will tell you if the chain is incomplete ("Chain Issues") and will try to show the missing intermediate certificates.

- How to verify a trusted Root-CA

  - SSLLabs will check if one of the common CA is used as the trust anchor.

  - 'openssl s_client' can check against a given CA. But it will in this case also check against OpenSSL default CA's too, so the result can be misleading.

- How to verify a client certificate

  - 'openssl s_client' can also use client certificate

  - Check to see configuration supports two way authentication

- How to verify which ciphers and protocols are supported by the server.

  - SSLLabs will show the available ciphers and protocols and also emulate the behavior of specific clients to see if a connection should be successful or why not. Please check that their tests use the same IP address as you do, notably SSLLabs currently does not support IPv6 addresses.

- How to verify if explicit TLS is used (STARTTLS etc)

- 'openssl s_client' supports SMTP, IMAP, FTP and POP3 with the '-starttls' option.

The tools and methods we have shown so far are usable on all platforms that run OpenSSL either from the command line or in some cases through a GUI. Public facing servers and clients can also avail themselves of the SSL Labs online testing tool, which incidentally also will test and certify your installation on a graded system.

There are other great tools such as Wireshark for troubleshooting the SSL/TLS handshake which unfortunately we do not have the space or time to cover in this book. But suffice to say that as Wireshark has dedicated SSL modules it can dissect and display the complex handshaking process in human readable format so is certainly worth downloading and playing with to see all the clear text negotiations that constitute a session's start and finish.

There is another widely accessible tool that we can use for testing and troubleshooting any SSL/TLS issues that is available for Windows 7 or above machines called Network Monitor.

Troubleshooting SSL in Windows

I have included these Windows specific commands from Microsoft TechNet for Network Monitor because if you are a windows user they are definitely of use when troubleshooting.

So to begin with let us start with a basic command:

```
NETSH TRACE START TRACEFILE=<FILENAMEANDPATH> CAPTURE=YES
MAXSIZE=200 FILEMODE=CIRCULAR OVERWRITE=YES REPORT=NO
```

Determining the protocol version is easily found by opening the packets exchanged in the initial hello exchange as this is determined during the connection set up.

Determining Client and Server in Trace

To determine which machine is the client and which is the server there is a simple command to determine which computer the source of the "Client Hello" message. That's the quick and easy way to understand who is initiating the conversation and which compute is the recipient of the session.

If you want to view of all of the client connections, then filter using just the Client Hello messages that way you can apply the filter:

```
TLS.TLSRECLAYER.TLSRECORDLAYER.SSLHANDSHAKE.HANDSHAKE.CLIENTHELLO
//TLS 1.X CLIENT HELLO FILTER
```

Finding SSL and TLS Negotiation Errors

SSL and TLS have a set client to server exchange where how the secure session will take place is ironed out and mutually agreed upon. This negotiation can go wrong for various reasons and the client or the server are allowed to send an error message to the other side of the conversation detailing that things went wrong. In SSL/TLS parlance this is known as an "alert" message. It invariably means that something went wrong. An example would be that a server side (Server Auth) certificate may be expired, or not trusted by the client, and the result is that the client would send a TLS alert message to the server. Servers can send the requesting clients TLS alerts for a variety of reasons as well.

This capture filter will only any TLS errors in the capture so you can quickly see if any are present at all...

```
TLS.TLSRECLAYER.TLSRECORDLAYER.CONTENTTYPE== 0X15 //THIS FILTER WILL
SHOW TLS ALERTS
```

If the server is perhaps closing the TLS session with a TCP reset after negotiation-without failing with a TLS alert-then you can help tune into that with a filter like this one, where we are looking for server side TCP resets and showing TLS negotiations as well.

```
TCP.Flags.Reset == 0x1 and ipv4.address==<IP of Server side> or
TLS.TlsRecLayer.TlsRecordLayer.SSLHandshake.HandShake
```

Keep in mind that TCP resets should always be expected at some point as the client closes out the session to the server. However, if there are a high volume of TCP resets with little or no "Application Data" (traffic which contains the encapsulated encrypted data between client and server) then you likely have a problem.

Today it is hard to believe that the SSL protocol has stood the test of time for over twenty years and not only survived but become ubiquitous and crucial to internet and web transactions. Yet, improper or careless SSL implementation is insecure breeds a false sense of security and a high source of vulnerability and risk. However, the risks and vulnerabilities of a careless SSL deployment are now more widely known outside of IT experts. Despite this SSL's potential failings are rarely acknowledged within DevOp environments where each discipline takes an isolated view of its importance.

SSL is still only one part of the overall Web security challenge. The core cryptography and key-exchange methods will always be the focus of active research to find new attacks and identify improvements, but the implementation details could yield the most improvements in security. End users will likely never notice many of these improvements, but they will need implemented by organizations, server operators and software developers in order to provide end-to-end security across an insecure internet.

Made in the USA
Coppell, TX
21 October 2020

40102368R00132